Aesop's Management Fables

Dick McCann and Jan Stewart

Illustrations by Sarah Ward

BUTTERWORTH
HEINEMANN

For Marian and Harry

Butterworth-Heinemann
Linacre House, Jordan Hill, Oxford OX2 8DP
A division of Reed Educational and Professional Publishing Ltd

A member of the Reed Elsevier plc group

OXFORD   BOSTON   JOHANNESBURG
MELBOURNE   NEW DELHI   SINGAPORE

First published 1997

British Library Cataloguing in Publication Data
A catalogue record for this book is available from the British Library

ISBN 0 7506 3341 7

Typeset by Avocet Typeset, Brill, Aylesbury, Bucks
Printed and bound in Great Britain by
Biddles Ltd, Guildford and King's Lynn

Contents

Preface

Animals' behaviour can so often mirror that of humans. Our realization that we could use these behaviours for management stories was serendipitous.

We wrote a frog story for a particular segment of a management development workshop to blend in with some creative visualization based on the sounds of a bull frog. This story, which is included in the book, was very effective in highlighting a major problem that many action-oriented managers have. It prompted us to write many more animal stories which have become this collection of 'management fables'.

We chose animals from all over the world to illustrate management problems; the kookaburra and wombat from Australia; the elephant, chameleon and weaverbird from Africa; the hedgehog and squirrel from the UK; and huskies, beavers and stagecoach horses from North America.

In formulating each chapter we decided to follow a teaching format that has been very successful for us. The first section contains an animal story, the second contains an equivalent management case study and the third draws out the major learning points.

In researching the fable genre we came across many examples of the way stories are used for teaching. We have summarized many of these and their principles in Part One of the book. After reading Part One, you may read the rest of the chapters in any order. Pick any animal that interests you and discover the application to the world of management.

C.S. Lewis said that 'we read to know we are not alone'. How true this is! Perhaps when reading through this book you will recognize managers you have worked with and maybe even yourself! For example, the wombat was written to illustrate one of our own management styles. (No prizes are offered for guessing who!) It is a favourite animal of ours and often misunderstood.

The original Aesop's fables were a collection of stories attributed to the Greek slave Aesop who lived around 600BC. Most of the characters are animals that talk and act like human beings and illustrate the failings and virtues of human nature in a simple, often humorous way. Perhaps the best known of Aesop's fables is 'The tortoise and the hare'. Similarly we have described the failings of managers we have met or worked with, by associating their behaviour with an appropriate animal.

Dick McCann and Jan Stewart

Part One

Introduction

Storytelling is an important part of everyone's life. Through storytelling we know so much more about our ancestors and their beliefs than we would without it. Stories celebrate achievements, inspire performance and capture cultural codes for living. They record human progress from the earliest days of civilization to current times, using both written and oral formats.

Everybody loves a story. From an early age children are entranced by fairy tales and fantasy stories. Go to a party and notice how everyone stops and listens to someone telling a story. Stories are a way of learning and in all cultures are handed down from generation to generation to pass on the collective wisdom of previous ages.

We have both conducted management training programmes for many years. When various models are presented and details discussed, eyes glaze over within a few minutes. However, when the same principles are illustrated by a story or an anecdote, the participants remember the story for years to come.

In this part of the book, we endeavour to share with you some of the sources of different stories and their history. What started off as a few stories written for special sessions on management workshops has developed into a major interest for us. We have used it as an excuse to spend hours in bookshops and libraries.

Introduction

Chapter One

Teaching with Tales

Fairy tales

Fairy tales often use magic and the supernatural to explain behavioural changes and illustrate the moral of the story. The magic wand is used in hypothetical questions in everyday life. How many times have you heard someone say, 'If you had a magic wand, what would you like to see happen?' I am sure many of us wish we had one!

Many fairy tales describe fundamental archetypes of the human existence – the heroic journey, despair, hopes, and methods for overcoming tribulations. In his classic book on fairy tales, *The Use of Enchantment* (1976), Bruno Bettelheim describes a practice in Hindu medicine where a psychically-disoriented person would be given a fairy tale on which to meditate. The fairy tale was therapeutic because the meditation helped the patient find his own solutions, through contemplating what the story seemed to imply about him and his inner conflicts at that particular moment in his life.

Fairy tales can also be a very effective technique to illustrate management principles.

Truth conquers all

ONCE UPON A TIME a wizard owned a magic factory. He paid his elf and pixie workers poorly, always promising bonuses when sales increased sufficiently. The cave workshop was damp and dingy. The work was strenuous, as the potion ingredients had to be collected each day and freshly ground. Training rabbits to secretly hide in top hats was also very challenging. Still, the magic made children happy and the workers thought the bonus would be a just reward for their toil.

The wizard was rich, but he constantly thought about ways to save money. He did not trust his elf and pixie workers and would eavesdrop by turning himself into a fly. One day the workers complained that the biscuits were always soggy, so the wizard immediately stopped the supply. The cave was too damp for biscuits anyway, he decided. He gathered lots of information from his secret visits but had to be careful. Once, in an effort to get close enough to hear, he was almost swatted!

One day the supervising elf asked the wizard for their promised bonus and told him the workers were unhappy. The wizard flew into a rage and turned the elf away, threatening him with dismissal. When they heard, the workers began to fight amongst themselves but then decided it was probably best to leave and forget their bonus. They would easily find work elsewhere.

In a land in the sky lived the Truth Fairy and she was sad to hear from her fairy helpers that the old wizard was ill treating his workers. She knew at once that she had to save the elves and pixies, before their families suffered.

The Truth Fairy knew the remedy. She flew down to the workshop and sprinkled her magic dust over the wizard. Almost immediately, he begged the elves and pixies to return, promising never to be mean and wicked again.

The wizard became a kind and generous leader. He paid the outstanding bonuses and refurbished the workroom. He even provided biscuits in airtight containers.

The wizard maintained his good humour even after the Truth Fairy's dust had worn off. To his surprise, the more generous he was to his workers, the more generous they were to him. Productivity increased. Before long he was a very rich man.

Would you like to know the secret of the Truth Fairy's magic dust? Maybe you might benefit from it too. Well, it is thoughtfully made with equal proportions of Tact, Respect, Understanding, Trust and Honesty. The fairy had found that TRUTH was the recipe for good leadership.

We crafted this story to introduce our TRUTH model of leadership on workshops. The TRUTH acronym is nothing revolutionary, but it is an easily remembered recipe for improving leadership. By weaving a story around the principles, they are easier to convey and more readily remembered.

Tact

The dictionary defines *tact* as a sense of knowing what is fitting and considerate in dealing with others, so as to avoid giving offence. It is also a skill to be used in handling difficult situations. Another word for it is *diplomacy*. Being blunt and getting straight to the point may have its merits in moderation, but when dealing with staff and customers, we would advocate *tact* in huge amounts. Most people respond better to criticism or feedback when given in a non-threatening, tactful way. Some people advocate openness when dealing with others and like to 'call a spade a spade'. An approach like this may be beneficial to the person delivering it, by allowing them to let off steam, but it can have a long-lasting, damaging effect on others. The skilful use of *tact* is an elegant approach to leadership which will generate *respect*.

Respect

The definition of respect is an 'attitude of deference, admiration or esteem.' *Respect* is a two-way process. Good leaders gain respect from others and also give respect to others for their knowledge, abilities and actions. *Respect*, once it is gained, has to be constant. People will make errors but if there is a high level of respect, they are more likely to be open about them and foster an atmosphere for learning from mistakes. Respect leads to *understanding*.

Understanding

Understanding is the 'ability to learn, judge, make decisions and also to be tolerant, sympathetic and wise towards people'. Making the time to *understand* the organization, its staff and its values will stand you in good stead for leadership. If you can learn *understanding*, in all its definitions, then *trust* can be established.

Trust

Trust is the 'reliance on and confidence in the worth and reliability of a person or thing'. Trust is one of the most difficult areas to address in modern organizations. It can only be achieved if there is *tact, respect, understanding* and *honesty*.

Honesty

This definition is the only one given in a negative format – it is 'not being given to lying, cheating and stealing'. Honesty does require a level of openness, but remember it needs to be tempered with *tact*.

These TRUTH factors are all inter-related, and provide the links which cultivate an environment within the organization to achieve its vision. Without TRUTH, strategic visions and missions are but words on paper. TRUTH is the link which allows the organization freedom to explore options, but offers security when changes create uncertainty.

A good analogy for these principles is that of the organization being the seedling and the TRUTH being the nourishment needed for the organization to grow towards its vision.

Stories from religions

In the years before Christ, people worshipped many gods and each god was responsible for some part of their life. Their belief in the gods helped explain why things happened. Without the gods, their lives would have held less meaning for them. They believed that their purpose in life was to serve the gods and in return they would receive plenty of food, many children and a healthy life. Such a purpose gave them the will to succeed.

To pass on the wisdom to future generations, the sacred story genre was established. These stories tell us who we are and how we relate to the world and our gods. They present images from the past adapted to the modern tongue and touch a deep unconscious chord within us. They have their own energy that can enter our inner self and connect us to a distant past and powerful primal forces. They convey a fundamental truth, a lesson, an insight or an emotion that resonates within us.

Greek mythology is rich in such stories and poets like Homer are famous for their recording of the myths. Many of the Nordic myths are well recorded too. Most cultures had a god, for example, who was responsible for the rain. This helped people understand why rainfall was intermittent. Only when this god was happy, did the rain fall and the plants grow. In times of drought, stories of displeased gods and wickedness by other beings stronger than the gods evolved. These stories were necessary to explain why droughts happened, so that the vagaries of nature could be understood.

This belief in the gods was handed down from generation to generation through stories and interpretations of events which 'proved' the gods' existence. Later on, but still in the years before Christ, the Greek philosophers attempted to prove that some of these explanations may be untrue. Their aim was to encourage people to take charge of their destiny rather than sit back and be victims of circumstances.

The early Greek philosophers said that Homer's recording of the myths gave the gods traits which were too human. They argued that gods were created by humans in their own image, rather than the other way around. Over the next few hundred years, the philosophers attempted to find natural reasons for events, rather than supernatural reasons. This philosophy was less magical for storytelling. It went into the realms of fact, leaving fiction somewhat in limbo for a while.

During this time the Dead Sea Scrolls and many other events recorded in the Bible show that the concept of several gods had been replaced by one god. However, unexplained phenomena were still recorded as supernatural rather than natural events.

The birth of Jesus and the recording of his miracles are the basis of Christianity today. Jesus was a very effective storyteller and he used parables as a way of showing how God is present in everyday life. He used images of a woman kneading dough, or a farmer sowing seed, or fishermen catching fish, to remind us that the divine appears in the most ordinary of daily activities. Jesus' stories could be understood by rich and poor, young and old. They all had an underlying message and were told to illustrate a fundamental moral theme.

All religions use stories as a way of teaching. As the Bible stories are usually well known, we often choose stories from unfamiliar religions to use in our workshops. Two of our favourite stories are told below. The first one is from the Sufi religion and is a good introduction to workshops on communication. The second one is from Zen Buddhism and is useful to introduce the concepts of work preference and work allocation.

The three deaf men and the dumb dervish (Shah, 1990)

Once upon a time there lived a poor goatherd. Every day he took some goats to a hill overlooking the village where he lived with his family, to seek fresh grazing. He was deaf, but this did not matter to him at all. One day he found that his wife had forgotten to give him the bundle containing his midday meal; nor did she send their child with it, as in the past when it had been forgotten, even when the sun was high overhead.

'I will go home and get it,' thought the goatherd; 'I cannot stay out here all this time until sundown, without a bite to eat.' Suddenly he noticed a man cutting shrubs on the hillside. He went up to him and said: 'Brother, please keep an eye on the goats and see that they do not stray, for my wife has stupidly forgotten my midday meal, and I must go back to the village for it.' Now the shrub-cutter was also deaf, and he heard not one word of what had been said, and completely misunderstood the goatherd.

He answered: 'Why should I give you any of the shrubs which I am cutting for my own animals? I have a cow and two sheep at home and I have to go far and wide to gather food for them. No, leave me, I want nothing to do with the likes of you, seeking to take what little belongs to me.'

And he waved his hand in derision, laughing harshly. The goatherd did not hear what was said, and replied: 'Oh, thank you, kind friend, for agreeing; I shall be as quick as I can. Blessings be upon you, you have set my mind at ease.' He ran off to the village, and went to his own humble hut. There he found his wife sick with a fever, with the neighbour's wife in attendance. He took his food bundle and ran back to the hill. He counted the goats carefully, and they were all there.

The shrub-cutter was still busy at his task, and the goatherd said to himself: 'Why, what an excellent person this most trustworthy shrub-cutter is! He has seen that my animals have not strayed, and seeks no thanks for this service! I will give him this lame goat which I meant to kill anyway. It will make a fine meal for him and his family tonight.' So, putting the undersized lame goat upon his shoulders, he bounded down the hill, calling as he ran: 'Ho, brother, here is a present for looking after my goats while I was away. My unfortunate wife has a fever, and that explains everything. Roast this goat for your evening meal tonight; see, it has a lame leg and I meant to kill it anyway!'

But the other did not hear his words and shouted in a rage: 'Vile goatherd, I never saw what happened while you were gone, how can I be responsible for the leg of your infernal animal! I was busy cutting these shrubs, and have no idea how it happened! Be off with you, or I shall strike you.'

The goatherd was amazed at the man's enraged gestures, but he could not hear what he was saying, so he called to a passer-by who was riding a fine horse, 'Noble sir, please, I beg you, tell me what this shrub-cutter is talking about. I happen to be deaf, and do not know why he has refused my gift with such annoyance!'

Both the goatherd and the shrub-cutter began to shout at the traveller, and he got off his horse and came towards them. Now, he was a horse-thief, and as deaf as a post, and he could not hear what they were saying. He was lost, and had meant to ask them where he was. But when he saw the threatening gestures of the other two men, he said: 'Yes, brothers, I stole the horse, I confess, but I did not know that it belonged to you. Forgive me, I pray, for I had a fleeting moment of temptation and acted without thinking!'

'I had nothing to do with the laming of the goat!' shouted the shrub-cutter. 'Get him to tell me why he will not accept my present,' urged the goatherd. 'I merely wanted to give it as a gesture of appreciation!'

'I certainly admit to taking the horse,' said the thief, 'but I am deaf, and cannot hear which of you owns it.'

At that moment an aged dervish came into view, walking along the dusty road towards the village. The shrub-cutter ran to him and, pulling at his robe, said: 'Venerable dervish, I am a deaf man who cannot make head nor tail of what these other two are saying. Will you please, in your wisdom, judge and explain what each of them is shouting about.'

The dervish, however, was dumb, and could not answer, but he came to them and looked searchingly into the faces of the three deaf ones, who had now stopped talking.

He looked so long and penetratingly, first at one, then at the other, that they began to feel uncomfortable.

His glittering eyes bored into theirs, seeking the truth of the matter, trying to get a clue to the situation. But each of the others began to fear that he was going to bewitch them, or gain control over their wills in some way. And suddenly, the thief sprang upon the horse, and rode it furiously away. Immediately the goatherd began to round up his animals, driving them farther up the hill. The shrub-cutter, lowering his eyes from those of the dervish, packed his shrubs into a net and hoisted it on to his shoulders, bounding down the hill towards his home.

The dervish continued his journey, thinking to himself that *speech can be such a useless form of communication that man might just as well have never been given it.*

The water-melon lesson (Hirose, 1992)

One summer's day Iemitsu (the Ruler) sent for Osho (a monk) and they passed the time talking about various things. He offered some water-melon to Osho: 'Zen Master, in the hot season fruit is best. Please help yourself to some melon.'

'Well, this is my favourite, thank you very much.'

When Osho saw the water-melon there was white sugar sprinkled on top of it. 'I shall help myself to it gratefully,' he said, and began to eat it avoiding the sugar.

Iemitsu thought this strange and asked him: 'Zen Master, you had better eat it with the sugar as I think it is sweeter. Why are you only eating the part with no sugar?'

'Isn't this water-melon?'

'That's right.'

'You offered me water-melon, so I am eating water-melon. If you offer me sugar I shall eat sugar.'

'What you are saying is right as far as it goes, but I thought it would be more delicious for you to eat the water-melon with sugar. So I offered it with sugar especially for you.'

'I cannot believe you are saying this, sir. Everything has its own special characteristic. Water-melon has its own taste and so, because I love water-melon, I am eating the part without sugar. However, eating water-melon with added taste is the same as using people wrongly by twisting their character, I think,' he said, giving a piercing glance at the people who were present.

Tribal stories

The still primitive tribes in Africa and other developing countries who do not yet use writing and books, pass on their traditions through stories. The Bushmen of the Kalahari and the Pygmies of Central Africa are prime examples. Their rituals and rites are all carried on through stories and songs, each generation learning them and teaching their children. Many of their rituals involve the elders telling stories. Passing on their knowledge is an important part of the survival of the tribe and their elders are protected at all costs.

All countries and nations have their own stories which they treasure and record. Some are richer than others, but all are important. In many of the Eastern European and Asian villages, even with education and printing available, there are still storytellers. These people have a very important role in the village and are known and respected by all. Their stories are often based on fact but have been adapted and embellished over the years. They attract an enormous following, both young and old.

An advantage of stories that are handed down by word of mouth is that they change to suit the needs and times of the people. The basic principles remain but the stories can be related to current events. If the stories are handed down in written form, they are often inappropriate to the current times and may therefore be misinterpreted or over-interpreted. The most popular versions of the Christian Bible are those that have been adapted to the language of today.

The Australian Aborigines still have their dreamtime stories, despite their culture being eroded by civilization. Many of the aboriginal tribes no longer keep to their traditions but have adapted to the western style of living. As a result some of their stories and language have been lost. Thankfully though, with education and modern technology the majority of the stories are recorded and published so that all Australians, and those interested in Australia and its culture, can share the rich heritage through stories. Although many of the traditions of passing on those stories have been lost, the stories themselves will live forever in books.

An example of one of the Aboriginal cautionary tales that has an interesting moral is published in a book called *The Opal that Turned into Fire*, compiled by Janet Matthews (1994).

Mundiba and the honey

A long time ago there was a great drought and food became very scarce. A group of people had their camp on the banks of the Culgoa river in north-western New South Wales. Some of them were too old and some of them were too young to hunt for food, but everybody needed it. All were hungry and worried for the water of the river was low, few fish could be caught, most mussels had been gathered and no waterbirds were attracted to this region. The Muruwari people shared their food with one another and, if the hunting or food gathering had been successful, the meal was enjoyed by everyone.

Mundiba was quite a young man and spent most of his time looking for the wild bees. He disappeared every morning soon after sunrise and did not return until sunset, invariably empty-handed, but he greedily ate his share of the food collected by the others. It seemed odd that he sometimes said that he had seen some nests, but like the other food, honey was in short supply and he could not find any. Among the group was a 'clever man' or gubi, who was suspicious about the behaviour of Mundiba. He decided to send his special singer, or spirit servant, to follow the young man on one of his expeditions.

The small, invisible spirit followed Mundiba and was behind

him when he came to the first tree that contained a nest and honey. He had to climb the tree before making a hole in the trunk with his stone tomahawk. This obviously had been made before, but had to be enlarged so that his hand could move more freely when gathering the honey. As he removed it, he was able to eat with relish the considerable amount of this rare sweetness of the bush, a procedure he repeated at several trees.

While Mundiba was up one tree and eating greedily, the singer started singing to persuade the hole to become smaller. The man was puzzled because each time he removed his hand after taking a mouthful he seemed to have to drag it through the opening. Soon it became necessary for him to put his hand much further inside the tree trunk. This time he could not pull it out and was stuck. His tomahawk dropped to the ground as he wriggled and he must have realized that escape was impossible without assistance. Some days later he was found dead, hanging by one arm from the tree. Quite often, old people explained similar strange events as the act of the 'little fella' or gubi.

The suffering and death of Mundiba was an example for later generations. His greediness, selfishness and refusal to obey the laws deserved severe punishment. Those who behaved in a similar manner could expect strict discipline which might bring death in unexpected ways and they were thus warned against all such misbehaviour.

This Aboriginal sacred story, whilst perhaps a little severe in punishment for the business world, carries a universal message of honesty and fairness, applicable to all facets of life.

True stories

Our interest in tribal stories brought us to read *The Forest People* (Turnbull, C. 1961). The BaMbuti are an African tribe living in the Ituri rain forests of central Africa. Commonly, we call them the 'pygmies'. The rain forests are dense and are essentially a vertical world. They live their life in surroundings where horizontals have little meaning and the concept of a 'horizon' is virtually unknown. The pygmies have become so adapted to their world – to the confines of familiarity – that when they leave it and enter other environments, such as the plains of

Africa, they become nauseous. Some will even collapse and fall seriously ill, if they are not returned to their rain forest.

Colin Turnbull relates a fascinating story about his BaMbuti friend, Kenge who struggled to understand the African savanna when exposed to it.

Kenge could not believe that they were the same mountains that we had seen from the forest; there they had seemed just like large hills to him. I tried to explain what the snow was – he thought it was some kind of white rock. Henri said it was water that turned colour when it was high up, but Kenge wanted to know why it didn't run down the mountainside like any other water. When Henri told him it also turned solid at that height, Kenge gave him a long steady look and said, 'Bongo yako!' (You liar!).

With typical pygmy philosophy, he accepted what he could not understand and turned his back on the mountains to look more closely at what lay all around him. He picked up a handful of grass, tasted it and smelled it. He said that it was bad grass and that the mud was also bad mud. He sniffed at the air and said it was bad air. In fact, as he had stated at the onset, it was altogether a very bad country. The guide pointed out the elephants, hoping to make him feel more at home. But Kenge was not impressed. He asked what good they were if we were not allowed to go and hunt them. Henri pointed out the antelopes, which had moved closer and were staring at us as curiously as ever. Kenge clapped his hands together and said that they would provide food for a whole camp for months and months. Then he saw the buffalo, still grazing lazily several miles away, far down below. He turned to me and said, 'What insects are those?'

When I told Kenge that the insects were buffalo, he roared with laughter and told me not to tell such stupid lies. When Henri, who was thoroughly puzzled, told him the same thing and explained that visitors to the park had to have a guide with them at all times because there were so many dangerous animals, Kenge still did not believe, but he strained his eyes to see more clearly and asked what kind of buffalo were so small. I told him they were sometimes nearly twice the size of a forest buffalo, and he shrugged his shoulders and said we would not be standing out here in the open if they were. I tried telling him they were possibly as far away from Epulu to the village of Kopu, beyond Eboyo. He began scraping mud off his arms and legs, no longer interested in such fantasies.

The road led on down to within about half a mile of where the herd was grazing, and as we got closer, the 'insects' must have seemed to get bigger and bigger. Kenge, who was now sitting on the outside, kept his face glued to the window, which nothing would make him lower. I even had to raise mine to keep him happy. I was never able to discover just what he thought was happening – whether he thought that the insects were changing into buffalo, or that they were miniature buffalo growing rapidly as we approached. His only comment was that they were not real buffalo, and he was not going to get out of the car again until we left the park.

Stories can have a powerful effect when the story content relates to a situation different from the one we are facing, but the message and underlying meaning are similar. The story of Kenge highlights the problems we all have when we are taken from our familiar environment and placed in a new one. Our confidence is shaken and often we struggle, as we attempt to adapt to the changed circumstances.

Kenge's story parallels the problems that many people face in their work environment. Organizations are changing rapidly as we find more effective ways to work and embrace the challenges introduced by the information technology revolution. Sometimes people have difficulty coping and, like Kenge, refuse to believe that their new world is real.

Using the Kenge story to illustrate the problems of change highlights the use of a technique known as a 'transderivational process'. The story becomes a metaphor for the problems facing an individual or group and a transderivational process is necessary to find relevance in the story. If the story is more obscure, then more 'work' is required to make the connection. The effectiveness of story telling to achieve lasting results is very much related to the 'transderivational gap' built into the story. This gap must be designed to meet the needs of the listener.

An example of how a story can work on a person at the unconscious level is given by Nelson Mandela in his book *Long Walk to Freedom* (Mandela, 1994). Mandela relates a story about his Xhosa chief's speech, after his manhood rites had ended in a ceremony in his township when he was sixteen.

The audience became more and more quiet as Chief Maligqili spoke and, I think, I became more and more angry. No one wanted to hear the words that he spoke that day. I know that I myself did not want to hear them. I was cross rather than aroused by the chief's remarks, dismissing his words as the abusive comments of an ignorant man who was unable to appreciate the value of an education and the benefits that the white man had brought to our country. At that time, I looked on the white man not as an oppressor but as a benefactor, and I thought the chief was enormously ungrateful. This upstart chief was ruining my day, spoiling the proud feeling with wrong-headed remarks.

But without exactly understanding why, his words soon began to work on me. He had sown a seed, and though I had let that seed lie dormant for a long season, it eventually began to grow. Later I realized that the ignorant man that day was not the chief but myself.

Learning from stories

When our children are young we tell stories to entertain them and encourage them to read. Many young children have their favourite stories which they like to hear over and over again. They know the stories so well that even though they can't read themselves, they know if the storyteller misses out a line or a page! The stories create a visual picture for them and missing out important details omits one part of the picture. Children's stories are written to stimulate their imagination and also encourage them to learn. The stories are not limited by fact and can incorporate many fictional concepts which would cause an adult to lose interest.

Children's imagination is unlimited, as they do not have life experiences to bring them back to reality. For them, fairies and elves and little boys who don't want to grow up are all acceptable. Their imagination allows them to indulge freely in these fantasies.

Apart from our love of management training and writing, we share a favourite childhood book *The Faraway Tree* by Enid Blyton (1939, 1984). We were brought up in different countries with very different lifestyles and education, but we both remember this book. We can vividly recall being totally absorbed in the lands at the top of the tree and with characters such as Moonface and Dame Wash-a-lot.

We both read the book to our children (whether that was for us or for them is an area for debate!) Nevertheless, it was an experience we enjoyed for a second time through their eyes. It was still magical, twenty-five years later.

This personal insight indicates how important stories are to child development. Even as adults, we love stories. One of the best compliments you can give people is to tell them they are wonderful storytellers. Witness those who can hold their audience spellbound in either a theatre or at a cocktail party.

Many people dislike television as it leaves nothing to the imagination. Research has shown that children who watch a lot of television lose some of their ability to use their imagination. The pre-defined image limits the fantasies that can be created.

Reading or listening to stories allows you to go where you want to go. Your imagination can freely paint a picture of any event or person described. How many times have you read a book and then been disappointed in the movie? Stories are exciting because you create the scene and are its sole spectator.

Stories are particularly useful in personal and management development, particularly when a story is chosen to highlight a known problem that the listener has. However, the process works best when the listener doesn't know that the storyteller is aware of the problem. It also works particularly well when the listener is not even aware that he/she has a problem!

When a story is told well, the listener is captivated by the story-telling process. However, at the deeper or 'second attention' level, a search for meaning starts, particularly if the story strikes a chord deep within the person. This association takes place as an unconscious process and some time later can burst through to consciousness, resulting in appropriate behaviour change.

Language

The language used is another vital part of storytelling. Using words which create a picture and allow the listener to believe in the event or the character of the person is an art. Over the years many people have developed a reputation for this skill.

Winston Churchill, who was the Prime Minister of Britain during World War II, was noted for his speeches. He wrote the speeches himself and they were rich in metaphors to create visual imagery. His message was always put across in simple and positive terms. He gave his speeches titles like 'Liberation is Sure'. His images created in the British public, a sense of belonging to a great nation. They felt that their contribution, however small, was vital to the war effort. The patriotic fervour that he inspired will be remembered in history for decades to come.

Examples of some of the rich metaphors he used in his 'Liberation is Sure' speech are:

. . . establishing order and freedom of movement amid the waves of anarchy and sea of murder. . .

If the light of freedom which still burns so brightly in the frozen north should be finally quenched it might well herald a return to the dark ages . . .

. . . the day will come when the joy bells will ring again throughout Europe and when victorious nations, masters not only of their foes but of themselves, will plan and build in justice, in tradition and in freedom, a house of many mansions where there will be room for all.

Summary

Story content and the language used are critical to learning. The best stories are those which have an underlying meaning, where a transderivational process is activated to release personal understanding in the story. In this book we have tried to do this for the important area of management.

Over the years we have both experienced good and bad managers. Some of the important characteristics of 'bad' managers have been crafted into our stories and each one has important learning points. By no means are our stories exhaustive about management. We have simply created a selection designed to present ideas and concepts in an interesting, memorable format. There are many books about managing, but how often do we forget what was in them? Hopefully you, the reader, will remember a few of the important principles through the stories that take your fancy.

But for now, sit back comfortably, relax, and enjoy the rest of this book.

Part Two

Animal Stories

This section of the book deals with individual managers and their behaviour. Each chapter is split into three parts.

The first part is an animal story. The animals chosen were those with characteristics similar to the manager being portrayed. The second part is a case study based on real-life problems that many managers face in their day-to-day tasks. The third part discusses guidelines that might be employed to overcome the managerial deficiencies described in the first two parts.

The two stories portray the same problems in different ways. The animal story uses a fantasy scenario with descriptive language designed to aid internal visualization. The management story is more of the 'case study' genre and has been written in a factual and credible manner suitable for practical teaching. The messages in each story are similar but the two different formats will ensure that the underlying meaning will be interpreted by most audiences. When using the stories in a workshop situation, a mixture of the two types can be used to ensure maximum impact.

The third part of each story makes the underlying principles explicit. For individual readers, our comments will enable you to reflect on your own management style. For workshop facilitators, the guidelines will help you lead group discussions for initiating behavioural change in managers.

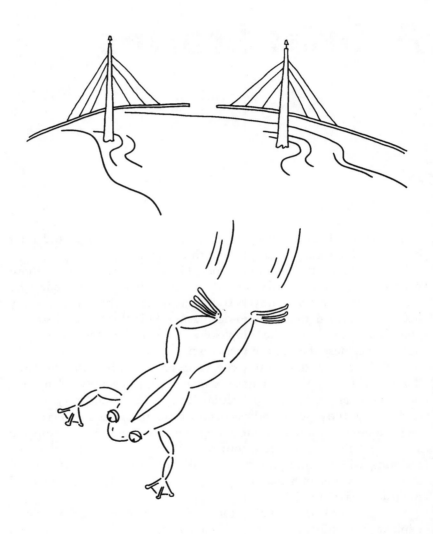

Chapter Two

The Frog

Life had been peaceful in the billabong. Everyone got on with their own lives. All were happy to believe that the world stopped at the edge of the water. Only the frogs came and went. Everyone else stayed happily in the warm, calm water. Occasionally, a new fish or insect would be washed into the little billabong from the small creek that kept the water fresh and moving, but little else disturbed their tranquil existence.

There were many families of frogs who lived in and around the billabong. They used the pond as a nursery for their eggs. The young tadpoles had a safe home in which to mature.

It was springtime. The tadpoles were sprouting legs and learning to leave the water for short spells. It seemed no time at all before they were perfect little frogs.

One of the young frogs was a lively, inquisitive green frog with the biggest eyes you can imagine. Now he was old enough, he spent his days jumping around the billabong, discovering all the interesting nooks and crannies. Their occupants were not at all pleased to see him, but he didn't worry about that. He was having fun. He liked to see where they lived and was quite unaware that his continual visits and interruptions were spoiling their once halcyon days in the billabong.

As he matured, he went on forays up and down the creek, poking his nose into everyone's business and making it difficult for others to get on with their daily lives.

One day he found this wonderful new billabong, where there was no-one else living. It was surrounded by large trees which let their branches dip into the water. He was enchanted. It was perfect for him and his young frog friends. They could set up a new home here without the interference of any of the older frogs.

He was so excited he could hardly wait to get back and gather his friends together. He hopped off home, his heart pounding with the great news.

On his return, he told all the young frogs what he had seen. He described this new paradise in glowing terms and persuaded them all that it could be their new home. They would have tremendous fun and he listed all the thrilling things they could accomplish if they were on their own. Convinced that he was right and this wonderful place must exist, the young frogs followed their new leader to the bounteous billabong at the other side of the forest.

They arrived and were delighted to find that the place of their dreams did exist. It was a truly awesome abode for the young frogs. Without hesitation, they jumped into the water and investigated all the banks looking for comfortable places where they could live.

Within twelve hours they were all asleep, never to awaken again. No one had thought to ask why the pond was uninhabited. Effluent from the chemical factory further up the creek contained poisonous chemicals which had polluted the pond, killing all the previous inhabitants. Had the young frog and his friends investigated further, they would have seen that the trees were dying and their branches were dipping into the pond as they wilted. The water was a mysterious, misty blue.

Look before you leap

Robert Bentley was a tall, angular man with a large nose and a keen stare. He was promoted to the position of operations manager and took with him a reputation for great organizing skills. Robert was a very structured person who could organize a project and set it in motion in the shortest possible time. In previous positions within the company, he had earned the reputation of being a good leader and systems expert.

As operations manager, he had to not only organize the project, but also assess its viability and see it through to the final stage. Each tender the company submitted was Robert's responsibility. He had two other managers who would liaise with him on the tender, but the final decisions were left with him.

His first tender was for the restoration of a bridge in a rural village. The bridge was built in the 1960s and needed painting and resurfacing. Robert and his colleagues met to discuss the tender. Despite objections from the other managers, Robert decided that there was no need for a survey, as the bridge was of minimal length and the majority of the data was on the old sketches.

The tender was submitted to the local council and approved. Robert was delighted. Now he could do the part of his job which he preferred. He put the task into action, organizing the latest state-of-the-art metal paint for the bridge structure, as well as the work teams to paint and resurface the bridge.

It wasn't until the teams arrived on site that the situation was realized. The bridge, although mainly metal, had at least 40 per cent of its structure composed of large wooden beams, to which the metal paint would not adhere. In addition, the surface was part cement, not completely Tarmacadam, as Robert had assumed. Robert's tender was much lower than the others and had been automatically accepted, as the company had an excellent reputation for superior work.

Robert was shocked that the bridge was not of the construction usual for that period. Had he listened to his colleagues and surveyed the bridge before making a tender, he would have prevented the extra costs incurred by the company. Robert was able to rectify all the problems that had arisen and quickly organized alternative materials to complete the contract within the tender period. His excellent organizing skills helped him pull the company out of the predicament without damaging their reputation.

The company, however, made a loss on the project. Robert retained his job but was careful from that point on. In future, he always made sure that he had all the necessary data before making decisions.

Frog managers

Many managers like Robert Bentley have frog-like tendencies. They forget the age-old advice to 'look before you leap'. Under the pressures of modern business where competition is keen, they have to make quick decisions. This need for quick decisions develops into an action-oriented style of management.

However, unless the correct information is gathered, then decisions will be made on incorrect data. Making assumptions based on minimum information, maximizes the probability of errors. It is important to spend time making sure that all data has been gathered and that any assumptions are based on facts. Time spent in gathering information at an early stage is often repaid many times over by a reduction in the number of poor decisions.

To do a job effectively, a manager must have access to all the relevant information associated with the work of the team. This means reading reports, books, journals and newspapers, as well as attending conferences and seminars to ensure that the team is up-to-date with the latest information.

Information can also be gathered through networking, where regular meetings are held with people from other organizations. This is why many people regard membership of clubs, professional societies, and business organizations as an important part of their job.

Gathering information can be very time consuming, which is why it is sometimes ignored by frog managers. However, the information technology revolution is changing all this and the challenge for today's manager is to master the rapid information explosion that is taking place through the establishment of such computer networks as the Internet. Learning how to use these systems will save managers time and give access to current information worldwide.

Tips for frog managers

In the short term

Use the 5WH technique (5 'W' questions and one 'H' (how) question) when faced with a decision:

- What information do you need?
- Why do you need it?
- Where will you get it from?
- Who will get it?
- When do you need it?
- How will you get it?

In the longer term

Get into the habit of:

- Setting aside time to read, research and be aware of the latest developments in your field.
- Allocating time to meet with others to learn what they are thinking and planning.
- Considering what information you should share with others to foster a good information flow.
- Consulting key stakeholders on any projects to ensure that their concerns and ideas are taken into account before any decisions are made.

Thought for the Frog Manager

Prevention rather than cure
Reduces the stress you need endure.

Chapter Three

The Squirrel

SAMMY SQUIRREL LIVED in St James' Park in London. It was a busy place with many visitors and much traffic noise. A lilied stream meandered through the park, providing a safe home for the eager ducks and graceful swans. The trees were well tended by the gardening staff, although some bored youngster might occasionally carve words in the tree trunks. In all, it was a lovely place to live. There was abundant food and the population of birds and squirrels were well-fed and healthy.

Sammy had learnt very quickly how to ensure a regular supply of food for his immediate needs, as well as his winter hibernation. He soon realized that humans were easy providers, readily falling for his charm. He would run down the tree and sit near them whilst they picnicked, cutely twitching his nose. Tasty morsels were propelled in his direction and sometimes he would be encouraged to eat from a picnicker's hand. Senior citizens were his favourite. Daily, he would look for them strolling in the park, following them to the benches they selected to enjoy lunch. This was his best source of food as many would bring him a supply of nuts from exotic lands. He would sit erect, holding the nut with his front paws and cracking the kernel with his teeth. This rehearsed manoeuvre enchanted the elderly audience and ensured they would return another day.

When he was bored, he would scamper off to the other side of the park searching for food to satisfy his winter hunger. He would hoard his supply in the cavity of an old branch, safely in the highest part of the tree. His store was enormous, but he had to be vigilant, lest the other squirrels, not as clever as Sammy, might raid his food supply whilst he was away 'busking'. To reduce the risk from pilferers, he found new caches in different areas of the park, thereby ensuring he would not starve during the long, bleak winter.

All summer Sammy weaved his magic on the park visitors. His storage areas were overflowing with food, far too much for him to eat himself or even for the other members of his family. This did not deter him as he was hooked on gathering food. It was an important part of his day and he enjoyed preening himself in front of his admirers. The members of his family tried to discourage him from collecting more food by asking him to give some of it away, so that the other squirrels in the park would have enough. Sammy was not at all interested. It was his food, earned by his own endeavours. Perhaps next spring he might give some away, if there were any left. He refused to listen and continued collecting, until nature told him it was time to retire for his long rest.

His coat was now thick and beautifully coloured red. His luxuriant fur would make him warm and cosy all winter and with abundant food, he could live like a king. He felt smugly satisfied that he had put his talents and the warm months to good use. He prepared for his slumber, knowing that his food supply would ensure he would not need to forage through the bitter, winter snow. To his horror, he discovered that much of the food he had gathered was rotting. He had stored so much in the small stores that air could not circulate. The nuts, fruit and berries were fermenting in the damp environment. Much of the food the humans had given him was also smelly and almost unrecognizable.

He quickly ran to his other store houses and discovered that all but one were in a similar condition. Waves of panic swept over him. Despite all his hard work, he would have very little to eat. Desperately, he rescued as much of the food as possible and brought it to his winter home. It was a meagre supply but with his thermal coat and healthy body, he knew he could survive the winter. It was a hard lesson for him but hopefully next year he would gather better quality food and not be so greedy. Perhaps a few humans would come into the park in the winter to leave him some nuts. He could always hope!

Information hoarding

'For goodness sake make a decision!' was a frequent cry to be heard in the offices of one of South America's larger rubber companies. Carlos Martinez had worked with the firm for nearly ten years and was popular amongst his colleagues. He had been a member of the research team which had successfully developed new rubber moulding techniques and had been recently promoted to the position of production manager.

Carlos was a wonderfully cheerful person with a happy smile and a word for everyone. He was said to be able to 'charm the birds from the trees'. He was a brilliant researcher and during ten years had developed many innovative ideas for improving the rubber production processes. His reward was a promotion to the senior management team.

Initially Carlos was delighted, as the promotion meant a higher salary and expenses to sustain his busy social lifestyle. His first task in his new job was to audit the production process and gather as much information as possible. He wanted to understand in detail what each person did and the processes used to progress an order through to delivery. Being a gregarious person he would regularly wander around the factory, chatting to anyone who had time to spare. Then he would return to his office and collate the information, making entries in a computer database program that he had written during his time in research.

Carlos was a member of several professional institutes and made arrangements to visit other rubber companies in Brazil, Argentina and Chile. He wanted to keep abreast of latest developments which he might be able to introduce to his production line. He also made contact with production managers in several petrochemical plants whose processes were similar to those used in the rubber company.

He subscribed to several technical magazines and regularly

visited the local and national libraries. Most mornings he would spend reading his magazines and two of the daily newspapers. Items that interested him were logged in his database for retrieval and analysis later. Most evenings he logged onto the World Wide Web, exploring the home pages of international businesses and professional institutes. In this way he would find out about overseas conferences on rubber technology. He used a considerable part of his training budget to ensure that he attended the more important events.

Meanwhile, members of the production team were becoming anxious. They had customers waiting for special orders, tenders to place for new business and production line problems to solve. Most of the decisions required approval from Carlos. However, Carlos was always too busy gathering information and had little time to analyse it and virtually no time to make decisions. When pressed for a decision, Carlos would usually say, 'I'll look into it'. Nothing eventuated and production was slowly grinding to a halt. Gradually Carlos' office became filled with books, journals, reports and newspaper clippings. Filing cabinets completely encircled his desk.

Carlos was oblivious to the problems he was causing. He believed that once he had all the information relating to a situation then the solution would be obvious. However, he was never able to make the final decision because he never seemed to have enough data! Often during departmental meetings he would refer a problem to a sub-committee, to ensure that adequate time was spent on obtaining the 'right' decision.

Sometimes Carlos' team had to by-pass him and go straight to the managing director. This caused tension within the team and undermined Carlos' position. Other managers within the company also begged Carlos for a decision, particularly with regard to new computer-controlled machinery. Carlos continually delayed his decision, waiting for a new model, which was always 'about to be released'. Carlos began to feel stressed, complaining that there never seemed to be enough time to do his job properly.

The situation became serious when a tender deadline was missed and a five-year contract went to a competitor. The directors wanted to know the reasons. Carlos tried to explain that he was awaiting some information on new colour-bonding materials and wanted to include these in the tender. He had overlooked the tender deadline. Carlos used the meeting to talk with the directors about his plans for the future. In his eloquent way he showed some preliminary results from a German university on cross molecular bonding and persuaded the managing director to send him to an international conference in Charmonix which he would combine with a skiing holiday on Mount Blanc.

Squirrel managers

To be an effective manager, decisions about people and tasks must be made regularly. Furthermore, there is usually little room for 'error' as wrong decisions at a high level have a big impact on the future direction of organizations. Good managers need to balance the quest for information with the drive for action.

Squirrel managers abound in the modern organization. Safely hoarding files of useless information they develop an inner satisfaction that they are working really hard. However, managerial effectiveness is usually rated on 'outputs' delivered, rather than 'inputs' processed. Squirrel managers fail to deliver results.

There is a class of people who are driven by the need for information. Rather than take a risky decision they will opt for a search for more data. There is a satisfaction and comfort for them in searching for the 'truth'. Once the 'truth' is discovered, they are happy with making a decision. They tend to be risk averse, wanting to be sure that each decision they take is definitely the correct one. If there is a degree of uncertainty they will seek even more data, often referring problems to sub-committees for further data gathering and analysis. Squirrel managers are a mine of information, but often it is a tin mine rather than a gold mine!

Proof that squirrel managers are plentiful, lies in many of the 'catch phrases' that describe them. Sometimes they are known as 'mirror managers' because of their tendency to say, like Carlos, 'I'll look into it', when pressed for a decision. Sometimes they are called 'boomerang managers' – 'I'll get back to you', or 'boat captains' – 'I'll take it on board' or 'card sharks' – 'Don't worry, I'll deal with it'. Most times these phrases are clues that indicate the person uttering them has no intention of taking action at all.

You can help squirrel managers be more action oriented by listening to the words that they use. Phrases like the ones above are known as 'fat and fuzzy'. When you hear them, try visualizing the words. For example, is the phrase 'I'll get back to you,' lean and precise, or is it vague and ambiguous? Your task is to turn it into an action that is clear and unambiguous, by requesting more information. Responses from you similar to those below may help:

'When will you get back to me?'
'Friday?'
'Before lunch?'
'Phone or fax?'

If you are a squirrel manager yourself, then think about the times you said you would follow something up but never did, because your need for information split your attention across many different activities. Next time you say, 'I'll look into it,' force yourself to follow up with a precise statement of when and how you will actually 'look into it'. In this way you will be making a commitment to deliver what you say.

There is no doubt that squirreling for information is an important part of everyone's job. It will certainly help prevent you from becoming a 'frog' manager. The secret of good management, though, is to seek the middle ground, ensuring that time is spent gathering information, but also knowing when to stop 'hoarding' and take action.

Effective managers have a certain degree of 'structure' in their activities. They have clear goals and objectives and a time by which these are required. Usually they will have established a number of 'key result areas', so they can continually monitor their performance.

Tips for squirrel managers

In the short term

If you have squirrel tendencies, you may need to review your management style. When faced with a new project or direction, write down the key information you require. Then divide the list into what is essential to know and what is 'nice to know'. Show your list to someone else and get their opinion, otherwise you might find that everything is in the 'essential' column. Concentrate your efforts on the essential information and then draw up a plan of how this information can be gathered in the shortest possible time. Check the resources you have to gather information and if necessary, like Oliver Twist, ask for more.

In the longer term

You may need to develop yourself to work in a more organized, structured way. This may take time and involves moving your focus away from 'information' towards 'implementation'.
- Try attending some workshops in the area of project planning, time management and quality. These will give you techniques to help you be more implementation-oriented.
- Look for people to work with you who are action-oriented. Listen to their advice on what information might be required.
- Try analysing your activities over a period of a month or so. Categorize your time into 'information time' and 'implementation time'. Look for a balance between the two.

Thought for the Squirrel Manager

*Gathering too much information
is a waste of time,
When important decisions
miss the deadline.*

Chapter Four

The Wombat

DESPITE THEIR REPUTATION for being muddle-headed, wombats are intelligent and gentle animals. Wallace was no exception. He lived in the sandy hills near the beach where the soil was easy to dig. There was plenty to eat as the moist air from the sea kept the vegetation damp and lush.

Wombats spend much of their day digging burrows. Their large front paws enable them to scoop up the earth which they toss behind them. Wallace would often experience soil showers as fellow wombats chose to dig near his resting places. But he was kind and gentle and did not worry. He would placidly lie there and allow himself to be covered by the dirt. When he was ready, he would stand up and shake himself. The soil was dry and soon fell from his soft brown coat. It wasn't worth getting upset about.

Wallace was rather partial to the succulent shoots of dune plants and he would amble over the sandhills to find the best ones. Some of the other wombats would see him leaving and trundle after him. They knew he was an expert at finding the tastiest roots and shoots, so they shadowed him closely. As soon as he discovered new growth, the other wombats bumped him out of the way and greedily ate the food. Wallace didn't worry; he knew he could find more. Friends were much harder to come by than tasty shoots.

Wallace was the best excavator in the colony too. He had a flair for finding natural weaknesses in the soil. Even though it was mainly sandy soil around the area, there were often seams of rock beneath the surface. These seams prevented the burrows being dug deep enough to protect the occupants from the predators and bushfires. He would help other wombats find a suitable place to burrow and then leave them to do the digging. His own burrow was almost 30 metres long with a cosy sleeping chamber. It also had a large entrance from where he could judge the weather and temperature before venturing into the evening air.

One day an emergency occurred and the wombats were terrified. Humans were encroaching upon the sandhills, driving long spikes into the ground as they surveyed the area for a housing estate. Many burrows had been pierced and one inhabitant had been killed. Wise Wallace would know what to do, so all the wombats gathered around his burrow. He had seen the humans on his wanderings but didn't realize they were now so close. Night was falling, so he advised everyone to collect enough food to last several days and then gather in the burrows furthest from the spikes.

Wallace ventured out early the next morning to see what was happening and, after examining the spikes, waited for the humans to arrive. Today they had brought large noisy 'monsters' with them and, for once, Wallace decided that the wombat colony was in great danger.

That evening he told everyone what he had seen. He said that the humans were here to stay and rather than risk their lives, they must relocate their colony. He would spend that night finding a new home for them.

He searched the whole evening for a place far away from the humans and the other wombat colonies which dotted the sandhills. He eventually found an ideal spot closer to the sea where his nose told him there were no humans within miles. He returned to his friends and led them to the new location. They all spent a busy night exploring their new surroundings and digging homes. Within two days peace had been restored. Wallace was again able to amble off on his own.

He was so glad that there was nothing to worry about. He

could now put his mind to creating his new burrow with all the comforts of his old one. He thought he might even dig a bigger entrance so that he could lay there sometimes and watch the world go by.

The reluctant manager

Sven Siebel was a brilliant man and liked by all. He had formed his own company on an innovative concept a few years ago and since then it had grown quickly. The company had a reputation for its excellent service and quality products.

Sven knew that he was not management oriented and tried a number of ways to relieve himself of the daily running of the company. He was a very trusting person and was happy to let the general manager, Anika Neeson, make decisions. He was interested in the monthly reports and kept an eye on the figures. So long as profits were being made, he did not interfere. He concentrated on the aspects of work that he enjoyed – researching new products and travelling overseas.

He kept his finger on the pulse of the company by meeting regularly with Anika over lunch. He enjoyed the relaxed atmosphere and decided that so long as the figures were good, everything else must be fine. He would occasionally visit the office and have a brief chat with the staff, but he never got to know any of them. He relied on the information he received from Anika.

Sven was unaware that Anika was very autocratic and liked to surround herself with sycophants. He saw a very different side of her in his meetings, as she was skilled in upward management. He was aware that there were a large number of dismissals during the past year, but he supposed it was usual in a small office. There was little room for promotion and efficiency had to be top priority to keep the customers happy.

It wasn't until the eighth dismissal that he decided he should investigate further. Upon interviewing the staff, he found that most were discontented and therefore he would reluctantly have to take a higher profile in the office again. He examined the figures in detail and, contrary to what Anika had told him, discovered that the sales were plateauing. Further investigation showed that Anika had no new marketing strategies, and that she rejected all input from the staff.

Slowly Sven reorganized responsibilities and engaged more staff so that a marketing and promotions unit could be established. Disappointed with the divisive rule of Anika, he reassigned roles and established a self-managing team. Anika resigned, as she could not tolerate the loss of her position and flatly refused to cooperate with the new management team.

Once the new team was in place and the first few meetings were successful, Sven bowed out of the office once more, leaving the team to decide the direction of the company. The team was not really strong enough to withstand this early pressure. Some members liaised with Sven on decisions, but others went their own way. The office was full of gossip and everyone felt that there was no direction. The staff enjoyed the flexibility of hours and freedom to make their own decisions, but they lacked a sense of achievement as there was no vision.

Sven was always available and responsive to staff requests, but he never insisted on meetings or regular audits, apart from the monthly report. Although the figures were excellent, morale was low and the staff who chose not to liaise with Sven were jealous of the ones who did. There was a lot of guarding of territory as there were no job descriptions defining who could do what, with which, and to whom!

Sven was reluctant to employ another general manager as he liked the self-managed team approach. He disliked conventional management structures and hierarchies. So he took the senior staff away on a team-building weekend. During those two days the team developed a strategic plan and created a vision for the company. Many grievances were aired and misconceptions dispelled. Back in the office, relationships were much improved and an air of cordiality returned. Sven was glad that everything was fixed again, so that he could amble off into his own areas of interest.

Sven's solution was short lived. Increase in business required more staff, reorganization and new directions. 'What a nuisance,' thought Sven. 'I will have to postpone this new book I am writing, and do everything over again!'

Wombat managers

Wombat managers are reluctant managers. They have the title and the responsibility but don't want to get involved with any of the problems; in other words they don't want to manage. Wombat managers often occur in small organizations where as the major shareholder, they are also the manager. In general they want a quiet life where they can indulge in those activities which interest them. They are too trusting and believe that if people are left to their own devices, they will naturally find the right way of working to achieve objectives.

Wallace Wombat had no real objectives in life. He lived in the present, reacting to any events that happened around him. He had a low threshold for action and often, it was easier just to allow fellow wombats to dump dirt on him, rather than complain or give feedback to them. Sven was also 'showered' by Anika and was quite prepared to believe whatever information she presented to him.

As a manager, it is important not to listen to just one person, but to 'wander around' listening to alternative views presented by everyone in your team. This is particularly the case in a management hierarchy where the information is often 'upward-filtered', so that senior managers are only told what they want to hear. The danger in this is that you will get to hear of problems before it is too late to take action.

Managers who just rely on bottom-line results are abrogating their responsibility as a leader. Excellent results can often be delivered from a team where there are severe relationship problems. However, the time lag eventually catches up, and sooner or later the problems in the team will manifest themselves in poor results. Waiting for the poor results before taking action results in a reverse lag. It is a while before things improve! A manager must understand the processes taking place within the team and take action before problems occur, rather than after.

All teams need objectives, a goal and a sense of purpose. Without them, organizations bumble along, living in the present and reacting to crises. While self-directed teams can be empowered to manage their own affairs, they still need a set of objectives which is aligned with the organizational 'vision'. In addition, they will need a lot of counselling and encouragement to be effective.

Tips for wombat managers

In the short term

- Don't allow yourself to be 'showered' by people you manage; listen to everyone's point of view and check the information you are given.
- High levels of trust are important but teams also need clear goals to prevent them floundering.
- Monitor your team's performance by establishing 'benchmarks' against which they can evaluate their performance.
- Establish clear quality guidelines aligned with customer needs and encourage your team to deliver them.

In the longer term

If you wish to be a wombat then you must take time to develop your team so that it is self managing. This will require you to establish a clear vision that is widely communicated throughout the organization and accepted by all staff. Next you must allow them to develop the skills they need to deliver the vision. Training and development and frequent coaching, counselling and communication will be required. This will initially occupy a lot of your time, but it is the only way you can make life easier for yourself in the long term.

Thought for the Wombat Manager

*Trusting staff is necessary but not
all they desire;
Give coaching and direction to complete
the tasks you require*

Chapter Five

The Elephant

I N THE HEART OF Africa lived a large herd of elephant. They roamed the vast expanse of scrubland under the hot, relentless sun. Each day, their routine was to visit one of the waterholes, to drink and cool themselves.

The leader of the herd was a large, majestic bull elephant. He had become leader in his early years of maturity, when the older leader had lost his life to a greedy ivory hunter who saw riches in his magnificent tusks. He had reigned supreme, defending his herd against all predators. Now in his later years, his tusks showed signs of many vicious battles.

He was a strong leader and unyielding in his decisions. He had protected the herd in his rigid way and had rarely listened to any other point of view. Often he would find himself in a potentially dangerous situation and have to make an immediate decision by himself. He had been lucky, on many occasions, not to lose young calves to the cunning and hungry lions.

The young bull elephants tried to encourage their leader to vary their routes and times to the waterholes, but to no avail. The lions knew the routines well and this made the calves easy prey.

Disaster struck! The leader missed seeing a lioness stalking the herd. She and two other lionesses leapt from the scrub, seizing two calves. Their mothers were distraught and fought valiantly to save their offspring. However, the lionesses were strong and determined, needing to feed their own young. They used the surprise attack to their advantage.

The leader flatly refused to believe that his decision not to vary the routines was at fault. After all, he had three wives whom he loved dearly. He would never jeopardize their well being. He believed he had the herd's best interests at heart.

The younger elephants again tried again to influence the leader into varying their routes and times to the waterholes. However, the leader simply would not listen. He continued to make his decisions as and when a crisis arose.

The loss of very young calves and the older, slower elephants to the lions became commonplace over the next few months. So the young bull elephants decided it was time their leader was replaced. The herd's young were sadly reduced and there was little hope of new calves being born in the harsh, drought conditions. The fewer the members of the herd, the more vulnerable they were becoming to attack, as the lions could sense their weakness and lack of unity.

The time had come to drive out the leader whilst there was still a herd left. The young bull elephants manoeuvred the leader into a dense scrub area and their strongest member engaged him in a raucous battle. It ended when the leader's weakened tusk snapped against a tough acacia bole. Defeated, he was exiled from the herd and left to roam the African scrub alone.

One-way communication

Eric Dilworth was the production manager of a general engineering business making engines and other parts for the automobile industry. He had been with the company for thirty years, starting his career as an apprentice fitter and then going to night school to eventually graduate as a mechanical engineer. His whole life centred around the engineering company and frequently he would arrive at work by 7:30am and still be there at 7:00pm, long after everyone else had gone home.

Eric was a forthright person and a decisive leader. Often crises would arise in the factory due to shortages of materials or machinery

breakdowns and Eric would swing into action, taking over from the supervisors and personally solving the problems. He felt comfortable in a crisis and a surge of adrenalin rushed through his body as he 'charged-off' to do battle with a recalcitrant supplier. On days when there was no crisis he would unconsciously create one, to give himself the 'high' he needed to feel satisfied.

Many of the supervisors and machinery operators found working for Eric very difficult, as he would rarely listen to them. He had an annoying habit of finishing off the other person's sentence for them and then continuing on with his own views. He would then present his solution and direct the other person to carry it out.

Eric never got his supervisors together for a team meeting. He thought meetings were a waste of time. The team members thought so too, because whatever ideas they presented, Eric would never listen, unless he agreed with them.

The main product for the company was a six cylinder engine used by several car manufacturers who adapted the basic design to fit their various models. The company could deliver an engine in three weeks, from the day the order was placed.

Several of the supervisors who had recently graduated had learned about 'just-in-time' management and also studied business process re-engineering (BPR). Two competitors were introducing BPR to their organizations and the supervisors tried to persuade Eric to support a presentation to the managing director on the benefits associated with BPR. Eric, however, refused to listen to their ideas.

Business started to drop away as competitors delivered engines in two weeks, rather than three, due to new information technology systems and the re-design of the organization to meet these needs. Employees were retrenched and most of the young supervisors left to join the competitors.

The company was eventually taken over by another firm which in five years had increased its market share from 8 per cent to 35 per cent. Eric was made redundant and replaced by one of his former supervisors who, two years previously, had left to join this competitor.

Elephant managers

Elephant managers believe in their own infallibility. Their ideas are 'right' and they think to themselves, 'How could anyone else know what to do? I am the manager and have got to where I am because I *know* what to do.' Consequently they switch off their attention and will not listen to what others are saying.

After many years of working with managers in the private and public sector we are convinced that the skill of *active listening* is one of the most important leadership skills. As one manager said to us, 'I am CEO of this organization and responsible for engineers, accountants, biochemists, physicists and a host of other professions. Most of the time I can barely understand what they are talking about. But I have learned to listen carefully, to seek clarification and to summarize my understanding of what they are saying. Then I can incorporate their views in my decision making.'

In the early 1980s the Sperry Corporation commissioned some research into *listening* as a business skill. They came to the conclusion that, despite its being the communication skill that is most used in business, it is the one to which least attention is paid by managers and leaders. Sperry's tests showed that immediately after listening to a ten-minute oral presentation, the average listener has heard, understood, evaluated and retained approximately one-half of what was said. Within 48 hours, the level of retention has dropped by another 50 per cent. In other words, on a good day we are likely to comprehend and retain only about one-quarter of what has been said!

In our experience, many managers are poor listeners. They do not understand the importance of focusing total awareness on what the other person is saying. Often they have several important projects underway simultaneously, and their minds are constantly racing from one project to the other.

To help explain the problem they have, it is useful to understand the 'word channel' model. The way we process auditory information can be divided into external word channels (W_e) and internal word channels (W_i):

$$W_e \overline{\qquad\qquad Auditory\ attention \qquad\qquad} W_i$$

Some people are naturally able to focus their awareness, without

interruption, on words coming to them from external sources (W_e). In other words they are naturally good listeners. Other people try to do this but their internal word channel (W_i) takes over and they complete the other person's sentence in their head and then run an internal dialogue (talk to themselves) as they think about the solution. When the other person pauses to draw breath, they are likely to take the opportunity to 'butt in' and verbalize their opinion. Their preference is to activate the internal word channel rather than the external one.

The problem is that the internal and external word channels are at the opposite ends of a continuum. When one is active, the other is likely to be attenuated or even switched off. People with a preference for the W_i channel have difficulty in activating their W_e channel and therefore they become swamped by their internal dialogue. In other words it is very difficult to listen closely to what someone else is saying if you are constantly talking to yourself!

So the secret of listening is to clear your mind of all internal dialogue and focus your attention on what the other person is saying.

You will notice when other people are not listening to you by watching their eyes. If their eyes 'glaze over' it is a signal that their internal word channel (or visual channel) has taken over and their attention is elsewhere. Physiologically the pupils dilate slightly and the focus goes to 'infinity' as the eye muscles relax. Whenever you notice this phenomenon, you must act to alter the pattern of non-listening which is about to occur. Almost anything you do that is different to what you have been doing will have a positive effect and bring their attention back to you. The *pattern interruption* can be elegant, such as pausing or asking a question, or it can be more overt, such as, 'Perhaps we should summarize what I've just said.'

So if someone is not listening to you, don't blame them entirely. Control is with you, as you can make them listen to you by skilful use of *pattern interruption*.

However, active listening is more than just taking in words. It is also about indicating to the other person that you have received and understood what they have said. Techniques such as seeking clarification, summarizing, and two-way discussion are all a part of the process of active listening. It doesn't mean that you have to agree with the other person; rather that you have heard and understood their message. In this way misunderstandings are avoided.

Hand-in-glove with active listening, goes the concept of participative decision making. Elephant managers do not like consulting others as they consider it slows down the decision-making process and indicates weakness. However, it has been shown many times that commitment to decisions can only occur when people are involved in the decision and 'own' the solution. It certainly slows down the implementation process, but time invested here is repaid with dividends later, as team members will put their heart and soul into making the agreed decision a success, because they are co-owners of the 'solution'. If a solution is imposed without consultation, many people will unconsciously oppose the implementation, passively working to ensure failure.

Two-way communication is a pre-requisite for good leadership. Nobody likes to be a mushroom (kept in the dark). Therefore a good system for passing information down through an organization is essential. People like to know what is going on, even if they don't necessarily need the information to do their job. It is the 'knowing', though, that leads to increased motivation, energy and enthusiasm.

A reverse flow of information is equally essential. Many of the best ideas for change and improvement come from those working in the 'front line'. Therefore it is a good idea to set up a formal system so that people have a means by which they can pass their ideas up through the organization. People will only feel confident about doing this if they consider they are being listened to. If the leadership is of the 'bull-elephant' type, the reverse flow of information will soon fizzle out.

Tips for elephant managers

In the short term

■ Set up a process so that your team members can feed back their ideas to you. Try setting aside an hour per month for an 'exploring' meeting where everyone knows they can explore ways of improving things.

■ Try the five-minute stand-up meeting each day to pass information down the organization. No one is allowed to sit down and the information is purely a top-down briefing. Each person then has a five-minute meeting with their team and so on. In this way people feel they are well informed, but the process does not waste time.

In the longer term

Develop the skills of active listening:

■ Be attentive to people when they are communicating with you.

■ Switch off your internal dialogue when someone is talking. Focus your awareness specifically on what they are saying.

■ Be congruent between what you say and what you do.

■ Check that the message you send to other people is received in the way you intended it to be understood.

■ Summarize the other person's viewpoint before you give yours.

■ Work out ways to involve all your team in key matters that affect them.

Thought for the Elephant Manager

*Why keep all the decisions in your domain and care,
When others have skills, knowledge and ideas to share?*

Chapter Six

The Cat

HERCULES WAS A beautiful, sleek, grey cat with huge, green eyes and a very haughty disposition. Hercules was only six weeks old when he joined the McNab family. He had been bought as a present for Connie's sixth birthday. Connie was delighted. She was the only girl in a family of eight children, and loved all animals. Mrs McNab was reluctant to own pets, as she feared that she would end up having to care for them herself. And she had enough to do already, with eight children and a husband! However, Connie had convinced her that a kitten would be no trouble saying, 'I am a big girl now and will look after it myself!'

Hercules was aloof, even as a kitten. Although he was playful at times, he often preferred to amuse himself, ignoring Connie. Undaunted, she would make toys to tempt him and would never tire of searching for him in the dense undergrowth of the neglected garden.

Hercules was a clean, impeccably-groomed cat who would sit majestically on the lounge window sill, watching the world go by. Connie would approach the sill and sit next to him, stroking his silky ears. He would immediately jump down and disappear. The rest of the family tried to befriend him and, on occasions, Hercules would allow them to stroke him. However, the boys soon lost interest; they would have much rather had a dog anyway. 'Cats are for girls!' they thought.

In the evenings, when Connie came home from school, Hercules would sit on her knee and purr softly. This was Connie's favourite time of the day but she was too young to realize his motives. Connie thought that he had missed her all day and wanted to be with her. Hercules, of course, was hungry but he knew that Connie needed to cuddle him first, or else he would have to wait longer for his meal. Once he had eaten, he then vanished until bedtime.

Later, he would turn his affection to Mrs McNab. He would rub around her legs and mew, whilst she tidied the kitchen before retiring to bed. He would tolerate her picking him up for a short while and then struggle free, continuing to mew. Mrs McNab knew he was only after a dish of milk before bed. She was a kind, loving person and couldn't refuse him one.

Hercules liked his family because they looked after him and gave him attention. But he didn't want to be stroked and petted. He had other interests in his life. Occasionally, he would want to be loved and so would choose the vacant knee of a family member to settle down for a warm sleep. As soon as he felt rested, he would jump down and leave the house through his special door. Mr McNab had fitted the door to eliminate the need to get up in the night to let Hercules either in or out, depending on his fancy. Mr McNab was a light sleeper and it always fell to him to deal with Hercules so that he could go back to sleep. Hercules would continue mewing and scratching at the door until someone paid attention to his needs.

Connie had bought Hercules a bell for his collar, as she disliked his penchant for the birds that came to eat bread and scraps from the bird tray she had placed in the garden. The bell was a nuisance for Hercules as it would scare off the birds before he was ready to pounce. After a few weeks, though, he learned to catch a bird without even the slightest tinkle of his bell until his prey was in his mouth. The bell then pealed its victory sounds as Hercules played with the bird until it was dead.

The birds were not the only victims of his stealth. He found that he could easily catch the fieldmice and small lizards which

lived in the McNab's overgrown garden. The lizards were his greatest challenge, as they insisted on losing their tails and escaping. Hercules seemed big and clumsy in comparison to their speed and agility, but he soon perfected his technique and added a smorgasbord of delicacies to his menu.

Hercules much preferred the fresh food he caught to the tinned, dry food that Connie gave him. As his skill increased, his intake of food from the McNab's pantry decreased. Connie was very worried at first, but after a while she didn't bother. Mrs McNab had explained that Hercules was obviously eating somewhere else because he was very fit and well. She didn't tell Connie that he was eating the wildlife in the garden. Connie loved all animals and would have been very upset.

Hercules was virtually independent now. He didn't greet Connie from school anymore and hardly ever sat on her knee. Connie had taken up netball with a local team and she trained two evenings a week after school. Now she was nine years old, her friends and outside interests occupied most of her spare time. Hercules was just the cat for her. He had never returned her love and although she would never hurt him and would cuddle him if he came to her, she had lost interest in him.

Aloofness

Barry Anderson was the commercial insurance division manager of a large international insurance company. He had a staff of around twenty-five which included two section managers and four process team leaders. He was a stickler for regular meetings which he invariably chaired. The section managers also conducted their meetings weekly and the team leaders met regularly with their teams as well. Barry's branch was the most efficient and productive in the company and he was justifiably pleased with his efforts. He worried about his staff and often fought untold battles with head office in their defence or to gain extra staff. He ensured they had the latest equipment and that they had ample training to be efficient in their work. He introduced new systems to speed up production and the branch always ran smoothly. However, his main concern was to look good in front of his boss, rather than necessarily caring for his staff.

Despite the success of the branch, Barry was a very difficult person to get along with. All the staff admired his knowledge of facts and he never attended a meeting unprepared. He spent hours poring over facts and figures and always knew the current loss ratios and other relevant information. Information was always at his fingertips and once he got the floor, he would hold it for long periods, expounding his theories and statistics. The meetings were much longer when he was involved, yet he would cut other people's contributions short, insisting that meeting times should be kept to a minimum. He was really only interested in his own solutions, and used the meetings to present his own ideas and get agreement.

He was very moody and for days would work in his office without stepping out of the door. He always worked long hours as he was unwilling to delegate. He felt that keeping much of the work to himself, gave him the edge on knowledge and with that came power. His other power play was to procrastinate on decision making when it suited him, and so put stress on his section leaders by his tardiness.

During his office-bound periods, he was unapproachable and would not even look up if anyone knocked on his door. The more insistent employees who needed decisions and information would be greeted with icy stares and short answers.

At other times he was chatty and would detain people in his office much longer than was necessary, not noticing their edging to the door to escape. He always had an opinion or view on every subject and would dominate the conversation. During his talkative periods he would demonstrate his knowledge of statistics, particularly concerning a current cricket match or rugby game. His statistical knowledge applied to almost anything.

Another characteristic which his subordinates found difficult to handle included his inability to stand by decisions made by his section leaders. After liaising with Barry, a section leader would make a decision on covering a risk requested by a major customer. The section leader would advise the customer who would be able to reverse the decision by telephoning Barry. This behaviour made the section leaders lose their credibility with major customers who would go straight to Barry if they didn't get the decision they wanted on a risk. The section leaders often acted as 'go-betweens' as Barry would rarely accept calls direct from customers.

Barry had strong beliefs about long lunches with customers,

often monitoring the time taken by team leaders. However, he rarely abided by his own rules and would frequently have long lunches, always claiming that they were in the interests of business. He knew everything that went on in the office and would always catch people sneaking out for a cigarette break when they had not removed their time cards from the bundy clock, as was the rule. He would notice all such minor indiscretions and then berate the section managers in a demeaning manner, for not watching their staff correctly.

Barry always led and dominated all conversations, whether it was business or one of the company social club functions. The main topic of conversation was usually work, or if other topics were raised he would quickly make a connection to insurance and his own work. On the rare occasions he asked about the outside interests of his staff, he would listen poorly and at the earliest opportunity regain control of the conversation.

The staff respected his technical abilities and the organizational structure of the branch, but none of them liked him and tended to avoid him whenever possible. The success of the branch was all to do with the design of its structure and nothing to do with Barry himself. The section managers were the ones who dealt with the team leaders and their teams and delivered the results. Fortunately both section managers, were highly motivated and skilled people who could mostly cope with Barry's behaviour. They had learnt the best ways to deal with his changing moods but looked forward to the day when he would be promoted to head office where his technical talents would be better suited. Dealing with staff and customers was not one of his strong points.

Cat managers

Cat managers were brought up in the old school of management. They are the boss, they have all the ideas, they have the power, and staff must bow down to their needs. Many of them are aloof, and when they want to interact with others, it is always on their terms. Many cat managers consider that people are inherently lazy and incompetent and need constant supervision; otherwise they will not do a job well. They manage by fear, constantly waiting to pounce on anybody not working to the rules. When they want to 'play', then it is always on their terms and at a time that suits them.

Cat managers demotivate staff and decrease efficiency by creating a negative environment where people put energy into avoidance behaviours. So much time is spent on protecting their backside, that eventually the work environment becomes an unhappy place and productivity declines.

Delegation is usually a problem for cat managers. Many of them have come from a technical background and have high skills in this area. Because of their knowledge they frequently say to themselves, 'By the time I explain to my people how to do the work, and then check that it is done in the right way, then I might as well have done it myself.' The cat manager ends up by working long hours and the staff learn to dump any problems 'upwards'. Why should they make a decision when the boss will probably reverse it anyway?

Cat managers need to realize that the skills required for technical expertise are often the opposite of those required to manage. Technical excellence usually requires long periods of working by oneself, researching problems, doing calculations and writing reports. Management involves setting goals and harnessing the resources of the organization to deliver these goals. 'People' are the most important resource and, like a machine, need attention. Successful managers may have to spend up to 80 per cent of their time just managing. Consequently work in technical areas must be delegated, otherwise neither the technical nor management areas of the job are performed well.

As we approach the next century it is clear that successful organizations will be those that empower their staff. People will respond to positive reinforcement rather than negative punishment and will lift their 'game' enormously, once they are given the chance.

The most successful organizations today are those that are customer focused. Customers want service and a quick response. They want decisions to be made on the spot by the representatives they talk to. Requests that have to pass up the organizational hierarchy for approval and then down again give customers the 'run around'. Before long they will drift to another organization that will give them the service they require.

Empowering your team to work in a self-directed way and make its own decisions will lead to increased customer focus. However, in such organizations there is no room for a cat manager.

Tips for cat managers

In the short term

- List all the positive and negative behaviours you exhibit in your team. Try to eliminate the negative ones and replace them with positive reinforcement.
- Try every day, to say something positive to your team members.
- Listen to your team members, rather than having them listen to you.

In the longer term

- Discuss with your team how you might devolve more responsibility to them.
- Ask others if they consider you to be aloof; if so then plan how you can spend more time interacting positively with your team.
- Review the balance between the technical and managerial aspects of your job.

Thought for the Cat Manager

Your team's respect will wither and die,
If you continually pounce,
dominate and pry.

Chapter Seven

The Spider

THE SPIDER FOUND a perfect place for her home. It was under the eaves of an old house and well sheltered from the weather, but not the passing insects.

She began to spin her web and worked quickly to complete the task, her mind constantly fantasizing the delicious meals she could expect to catch. At first her web was small, as she concentrated on strong foundations. Then she constructed the radial arms and began to weave an enormous expanse of intricate spun silk. The web shimmered in the sunlight as it spread out in all directions.

By early evening, the web was finished. As the insects emerged to enjoy the dusk, she was awaiting her first victims, smug in her superior lair. Hundreds of midges and winged ants flew by that evening and many of them were captured by the web. She paralysed them with her venom and moved them to her store house at one end of the web. This was her best haul for a long time. She had more food tonight than she could eat in a week.

However, this spider was greedy! In her selfish desire to look after her own needs she had ignored the other spiders who had been living under the eaves long before her. Her web was purposely spun over the top of their webs so as to intercept most of the insects. Only a few penetrated her threads to be caught in the other webs.

At first the other spiders tried to damage her web but she would mend it quickly and damage their webs in return. She was fearful that someone would take over her position in the eaves and guarded her territory zealously.

Each time her web needed repairing, she would strengthen the edges and extend them a little further, slowly encroaching upon the territory of other spiders. They soon gave up and moved on, leaving her to reign supreme.

Her enormous web was hard to maintain. Each night twenty to thirty insects were caught and these placed an immense strain on the fibres. They began to sag and eventually broke in several places. The dry summer weather was also affecting her web as the dust hung heavily on the sticky silk threads.

Eventually, the web broke and became impossible to repair. She would have to abandon it and start all over again in a new location.

Weaving a web

Ashleigh Smythe had been with the company from its first year of operation. She had no formal qualifications but had eventually risen to be a section manager, by virtue of her experience. Now she was in charge of the customer service area and guarded it jealously. She was always reluctant to share any information with the rest of the organization. She told people what she thought they needed to do to complete their job, but never revealed her own job to them.

Ashleigh knew most of the customers well and kept many of the details about their accounts in her head. Consequently whenever she was absent, the office was thrown into turmoil trying to service the customers' needs.

Ashleigh was worried about her status in the company as her own educational qualifications were inferior to those of the other section heads. She decided long ago that the way to make herself indispensable was to keep as much information and knowledge as possible to herself. She never taught anyone about account management or revealed the special information she had accumulated over the years. This made her feel powerful in the organization and removed the threat of others attempting to usurp her position.

Ashleigh was ambitious and wanted to be department manager. She viewed the other three section leaders with suspicion and considered them to be competition. Rather than cooperating with them to create a high-performing departmental team, she was constantly looking at ways to make them look bad.

One section leader was responsible for computer information systems, another marketing and the third for technical support.

A new computerized information system had been installed by the computer section and Ashleigh had been part of the project team. However she was reluctant to transfer the customer records to the new system as it might mean a loss of power. She failed to cooperate fully with the installation team and began to spread rumours that the new hardware was inadequate and that the wrong software package had been chosen.

Ashleigh now concentrated on the marketing manager. He was responsible for promoting and marketing the company's services to clients. When sales increased she claimed it was due to the effort put in by the customer services team, whereas it was largely due to effective marketing. When sales decreased, she produced figures from her customer records showing that the promotions campaign was inefficient.

The technical support section leader was responsible for advising customers and dealing with their technical problems. However, since Ashleigh was responsible for sales and servicing, she gradually started to answer their technical enquiries as well, indicating that she knew as much as, if not more than her section leader colleague.

The stress of the job slowly became too much for her. Customers phoned her about technical issues, suppliers contacted her about graphic design and printing and computer manufacturers plagued her with their products. Each day she would leave the office late and each morning she would be in first to try to catch up on the backlog of work.

The department began to suffer the effects. Although the customers had their orders, there were more mistakes and the filing was not up to date. Many of the other functions that Ashleigh kept for herself were being neglected. The monthly report would finally be finished in the middle of each month and some of the archiving had not been touched for months.

Spider managers

Spider managers create many inefficiencies in organizations. They spin their web into areas which are not their responsibility and as a result are unable to focus on the critical aspects of their own work. Further inefficiencies are created by the interference effect they have on others.

Many spider managers desire organizational power. Power comes in four basic forms:

- **Knowledge power** – this is wielding power by gathering and withholding *knowledge*.
- **Expert power** – this form of power is influencing others by being an *expert* in a particular field.
- **Position power** – this form of power is held by virtue of your position in the management hierarchy. If you manage people by indicating that you are the boss, then you are likely to be using *position* power.
- **Personal power** – if you exert influence because of the personal processes you use with others, then you are using *personal* power.

Spider managers specialize in knowledge power. By gathering knowledge from wherever they can and withholding it from others, they develop the power they crave. This makes them feel important and satisfies their need for power. Many of their activities are non-productive and the effectiveness of others is reduced. As a result the overall outputs of the team are reduced.

We have worked with many teams led by spider managers and the common characteristic is one of poor 'linking'. Very often there are no channels for information flows and every problem, idea or solution has to be approved by the leader. In terms of a 'linking' diagram, a team led by a spider manager often looks like Figure 1 rather than Figure 2.

In Figure 1 all the information flows are centred on the leader. In teams that are led this way, it is only the leader who knows what is

going on. One team member doesn't know what
another is doing. The result is a group of
individuals doing what the leader wants, rather
than a high-performing team harnessing the
synergy of teamwork. In Figure 2 we have a well
linked team where the information flows don't
necessarily pass through the leader. Informal
linking is encouraged and knowledge is freely shared.

The most effective power in leadership is that of personal
power. Personal power motivates others; it fills them with energy and
commitment to give of their best. Team members admire and respect
their leader and appreciate the skills he or she has in listening,
communicating and influencing. They feel they are consulted and
involved in the problem solving of key issues.

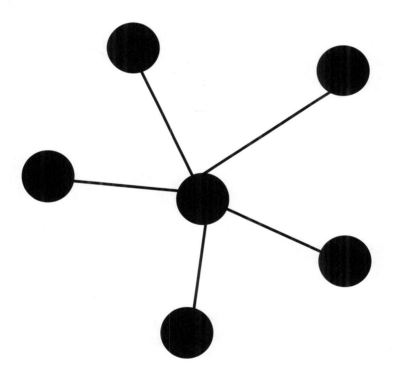

Figure 1 Poor linking

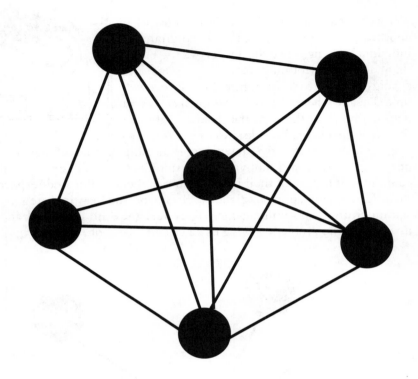

Figure 2 Good linking

Tips for spider managers

In the short term

■ Consider whether you are withholding information from others. Do you purposely intercept data and keep it to yourself? If so, you may be regarded as a 'spider' by your colleagues.

■ With the help of your team members, draw up a linking diagram, representing the strengths of the links by lines of varying thickness. If there are uneven links it could be evidence that you or other team members might be developing 'spider' tendencies. Consider what action you might take.

■ Rank in order the way you use the four forms of power. The key to success as a leader is in developing personal power. How can you develop these skills?

In the longer term

Often spider tendencies originate from a lack of confidence, experience or ability. A strong hold on all the knowledge breeds a sense of confidence and self esteem for the individual, but it is destructive for the team. Audit your own skills and decide how you can improve the areas of obvious weakness. Try also to develop a sense of openness with your colleagues. A free flow of information through regular exploring meetings will sweep away any cobwebs that might be forming.

Thought for the Spider Manager

Keeping knowledge from colleagues will cause distress;
Involving others and sharing is a recipe for success.

Chapter Eight

The *Chameleon*

I N THE LEAFY forests of southern Africa lived a colony of chameleons. These lizards are unique among reptiles, with their prehensile tail and tongue. They also have longer legs than normal lizards, which helps them in their treed habitat.

These chameleons were well adapted to their environment, but their numbers were rapidly depleting. They seemed to be such an easy meal for their predators. For centuries they had lived in their lush forests and no-one had ever considered moving. Increasingly, their lives had become more restricted and most of the day was spent hiding under large leaves. Rarely did they venture far from their familiar surroundings. Food collection was very difficult as they were unable to forage for long spells in the open. Their predators, however, were ever increasing in numbers as their food supply was easy and plentiful.

Occasionally, some chameleons had suggested that they should move from their forest and live in a safer place, but the main consensus of opinion was, 'We've been here for thousands of years so why bother changing?' As they aged, the older chameleons relied on the quicker, younger ones to gather food for them.

One day a youthful, adventurous chameleon decided that it was time for a new home. He was not prepared to wait to be eaten. He decided it was better to die trying for a better life, rather than waiting around to be someone's dinner.

So every day he would venture further afield, gathering as much information about the world outside the forest. He found that if he kept in the leaves, the predators were unable to see his bright green colour, but as soon as he was out in the open his movement was spotted against the brown soil, and he had to quickly run for cover again.

To his surprise, he found that when he stayed for a while in the open, his skin slowly changed colour to be more like the brown surroundings. Experimenting more, he found that, like a magician, he could change his skin to all sorts of colours, as it was exposed to the sun, to filtered light and to darkness. This colour change helped him enormously as he explored all sorts of new places. He cunningly learned to use it to his advantage. He would crawl to the edge of the foliage, stand still for a while and then gently rock to and fro to see if his movement alerted any predators. This motion gave his skin a chance to be exposed and adapt to the changing light. He would then be free to walk quickly across the soil, sand, dead leaves, or grass, knowing that his skin colour would now blend in with his surroundings.

He was extraordinarily pleased with himself, that he, and he alone, had found out about his amazing body. He spent weeks perfecting his colour changes and then returned to the colony to teach the other chameleons the secrets of camouflage.

However, it was not as easy as he had supposed. Very few were willing to risk trying out his new methods. They were afraid to expose themselves unnecessarily to danger. Most of them agreed that if they stayed where they were, in familiar surroundings, then they would have a better chance of survival.

The young chameleon was very disappointed and, far from being hailed as a hero, he was condemned as a fool. He had to think up better ways of convincing his colony that moving out and exposing their skins to light was the only hope for survival.

He spent hours with his friends and relatives telling them about life outside the forest. He explained how his discovery of their skin colour change was far more important than their unique tails and tongues.

Eventually, he managed to convince a few of the chameleons to go with him and experience life outside. The small band set off hesitantly, ever fearful of attack. Slowly their confidence grew and it wasn't long before they had mastered their new technique.

Unanimously, they decided to stay in the new habitat where they could gather food more easily. They felt less vulnerable, as they could scarcely be seen on the many different ground covers.

Now that he had convinced some of his friends, the young chameleon went back to the colony again, to convert the others to this new way of life. They refused to believe what he said and thought the others were all dead as none of them had returned. They accused him of being dangerous and disruptive to the colony and drove him out. They preferred to stay as they were!

Reluctantly, the young chameleon returned to the new colony and settled into daily life. Before long, the colony was flourishing. Their young were born in large numbers and their new lives were easier and fulfilling.

However, the young chameleon still worried about the colony in which he was born. Their numbers now were so few that their survival was doubtful but still they refused to believe that they could be saved by their skin!

Introducing change

Liz Moffat was a director of a small human resources organization selling management training products. With her two partners, she had founded the business three years ago and it had rapidly grown to a stage where its turnover was around one million pounds. Liz was outgoing and highly creative, with a quick eye for a business opportunity. Although she sometimes worked in a disorganized manner, she was constantly looking for new ideas and products as she knew that changing to meet customer needs was essential to survival in this business.

Although Liz had the vision to establish a company concentrating on supervisory training techniques, the success of the business was largely due to Jim Quiggley who as managing director turned Liz's ideas into reality. Jim had made the company very profitable by focusing on the existing products and marketing them extensively to supervisors and junior management.

Jim worked daily with his staff, trying to meet budget forecasts, but Liz had a roving remit to develop new business. Liz had the ability to focus on the future and could see where the organization might be in five years' time. Her vision for the future was developed by constantly attending conferences and meeting key people throughout the world. Sometimes the staff would joke about Liz not knowing the meaning of 'work' as they saw her continual visits away from the office as 'a holiday'.

Liz would return to the organization full of enthusiasm and speak eloquently about the changes that should be introduced in order to keep up with the latest trends. Jim and the staff would always react by giving reasons why her ideas would never work. 'Don't you understand,' they would say, 'that it takes at least three years and a lot of work to introduce a new product. We are better off concentrating on what we know well.'

To a large extent Liz was kept under control by Jim, but when she sensed her ideas were not gaining acceptance she would regularly talk to the staff, trying to persuade them of the benefits to be gained by changing direction and getting on the 'bandwagon' of the latest management training techniques. Many of the staff felt threatened by Liz's approach, particularly when she began explaining the staff savings that could be made by marketing a range of computer self-scoring instruments via the Internet. Many of them worried that their jobs might disappear. Consequently they became very negative to Liz's ideas and, as a result, vigorously opposed any ideas that she presented to them.

The reaction of Jim's staff to Liz caused him to become impatient with her constant call for change and he too became more negative, often saying to her, 'Oh no, not another bright idea.'

Finally the situation deteriorated and Liz decided that it was time to move out. Now anything that she presented for consideration was rejected by the board of directors. She sold out her interests and founded a new company to market new electronic training products that she had discovered on a recent trip to the USA. She convinced some of the staff to join her in her new venture. The idea was radical but survival in business was dependent upon rapid change to keep pace with competitors.

Chameleon managers

The greatest challenge to managers today is 'change' and how to deal with it. Recently we met the director of sales of one of the world's largest wineries who said, 'My job is so difficult. We cannot continue to do this year what we did last year. Consumer tastes are constantly changing and if we don't meet them, then we won't be the world's largest wine company.'

Change occurs at the fastest rate in high-technology organizations. In many of the top computer companies, 50 per cent of their sales relate to products that were commercialized only two years previously. Managers of these organizations are 'managing on the precipice', constantly having to adapt and modify their approach to match customer needs.

Chameleon managers understand the need for change and are constantly advocating it. However, they fail to realize that many people are uncomfortable with change and at the second attention or subconscious level will often go out of their way to prevent it from happening. When a familiar environment or 'habitat' is built up over many years it is easier to stay doing 'what we have always done'.

Managers who are successful in implementing change sell their ideas to others and gain commitment. To do this well, they take time to understand people and the different ways they process information and make decisions. It is particularly important to understand how people deal with the past, the present and the future – how they cope with their personal time history.

Chameleon managers tend to have 'time lines' which run at right angles to their body. The past is behind them, the present is in them and the future stretches out in front of them. Therefore, they can only see the future. Their whole orientation is future-based and this is the way they attempt to communicate their vision to others. Their language is often full of future-oriented, visual words. 'Can't you see how great it will be? Just picture our company in five years from now.' For them, the past is difficult to remember and you may even hear them say, 'Let's put the past behind us.' Some chameleon managers can barely remember what they did last week!

Other people have 'time lines' that do not intersect their body but lie in front of them. Stretching out before them, from left to right or right to left, is the past, the present and the future. Whenever they look to the future they can see in their peripheral vision, the past, and the present. Therefore to accept any future 'change', they need to understand how the future relates to the present and the past. For these people it is important to explain the change that is required and show that it is merely an extension of what has been done in the past and the present. If the change can be broken down into steps (like steps on a staircase), with each step being an incremental change from the next, then these people will see the pathway from where they are now to where they should be. Saying, 'Just picture our organization five years from now,' will excite a future-based person, but have little effect on a past-present person.

Communicating change to others is a skill that requires an understanding of people and how to influence them. Some people talk more slowly than others and therefore it is important to slow down your speech when influencing them. With others you may need to speed up, in order to capture their attention. Some people only respond when the *details* are presented to them and therefore appreciate written information to digest. Some people only accept information based on analytical reasoning. Others will reject any proposals that conflict with fundamental beliefs. Therefore the chameleon manager must be a master of communication, particularly the techniques of *pacing* and *leading*. These are discussed in detail in the book *How to Influence Others at Work* (McCann, 1993).

Tips for chameleon managers

In the short term

■ Take time to explain to others the pathway from where they are now to where they could be. Break everything down into incremental steps.

■ Carefully consider the impact that any change might have on others and be sensitive to their reaction.

In the longer term

Think about the various people with whom you work. They will all have differing ways of interpreting the world and will respond differently to the messages you transmit. Learn how to present the same message in many different ways. Eventually you will find a way where they may appreciate the benefits of your ideas.

Thought for the Chameleon Manager

Introduce change in such a way
That everyone wants to do
what you say.

Chapter Nine

The Cuckoo

CUCKOOS ARE UNIQUE amongst the birds of the English countryside. Folk tales say that the first signs of spring are heralded by the cuckoos' cries, as they return to England's shores at the beginning of the milder weather.

Cora was no exception to the rule. She was pleased to be back in England as the countryside began to awake. Food was plentiful this year and it wasn't long before she found a mate. She scoured the hedgerows to locate suitable nests in which to lay her eggs. These nests had to be of the right size as her eggs were quite large in comparison to many other native birds.

Now Cora had been mated, her fertilized eggs were ready to be laid. She had to be careful as she had to lay them undetected. Cora hid in the foliage until both occupants of the nest had flown off to collect food, leaving their own eggs unprotected for a short while. This was just long enough for Cora to settle into the nest and deposit her own egg amongst the others. She then flew off to the next nest. The occupants returned and settled back down onto their clutch of eggs, unaware that they had an extra egg to look after.

Cora laid an egg into three different nests. The parents treated it as their own, dutifully keeping it warm until hatching was complete. The baby birds were demanding from the first moment they broke forth from their shells. The parents flew far and wide to gather food for all the chicks. The young cuckoo grew much faster than their natural offspring and soon dominated the nest. The parents could barely meet the food demands of their insatiable foster child.

Cora was oblivious to the hardship she caused the foster parents, as her natural instincts told her to simply dump her egg in any nest that seemed suitable. After that her job was done. Meanwhile the foster parents struggled to provide the required care and attention for the fledglings. As the days passed, they made longer and longer journeys searching the countryside for new food sources. They grew very weak, but their sense of duty never wavered, even when some of their own fledglings were pushed out of the nest by this large 'gate-crasher', to die at the base of the tree.

Cora didn't stay around to see if her progeny survived. She had done her duty and she flew off to warmer climes to spend the rest of the summer building up her strength for the long migration and next year's breeding season.

Dumping the problem

Christa Van Rensburg ran a leading fashion house in Europe. It specialized in individual designs and was proud of its reputation for unique styling and personal service. Many of Europe's most influential women insisted on being dressed by Christa as she had an eye for good design and had cultivated a high profile throughout Europe.

Christa was constantly on the look out for emerging designers. If she was interested in their ideas, she would harness their expertise into her network and contract them to produce distinctive attire for the rich and famous.

Christa had not succeeded as a designer herself, as she lacked the discipline to follow through with her ideas and produce something truly unique. She had achieved success by building an efficient business that some would say exploited the talents of young designers.

Christa was outgoing and loved interacting socially with her clients. She continually met new customers who wanted something eye-catching for the next summer season. She would listen to the clients' general ideas and then contract one of her designers to produce an innovative and single make garment with little further supervision. Their designs were the property of the fashion house and they received very little credit for their hard work. Christa had to retain this copyright as her clients demanded their dresses be unique.

The initial contract had seemed a wonderful opportunity to be recognized in the fashion world, but in reality it was demanding work with little reward. If the client was satisfied, Christa took all the credit, indicating that the design was all hers and that the junior designer had merely carried out her instructions. If the client was unhappy or complaints made, Christa would immediately dump the problem on the designer to solve. The designer would then have to meet with the client, listen to her criticisms and placate her. Often a totally new design might need to be developed and Christa would insist that the designer take financial responsibility for the extra work.

The designers were continually under threat of losing their contract with Christa and having their reputation destroyed. Christa was a ruthless business woman who exploited her designers. She often said they were only as good as their last design. She took no responsibility for any failure and laid all blame squarely at the feet of the designer. In some instances she had even exposed the criticized designer to the media, setting back his career for years. Designers who were successful were eventually able to design under their own name, but Christa extracted a hefty commission for the recommendations she gave.

Cuckoo managers

Cuckoo managers are usually highly energetic people who are constantly thinking of new ideas. They seek contact with many people who continually give them insights into all sorts of possibilities. Their minds are constantly abuzz with ideas as they see opportunities everywhere. They are often described as people with 'many balls in the air' and may therefore have difficulty in juggling their priorities. Characteristically they dump their ideas and problems onto others so they are free to exercise their preference to look for the next exciting opportunity or deal.

In general, cuckoo managers are good at delegating. As soon as ideas or problems arise they are quickly delegated to others, with little pre-warning or understanding of the work involved. The cuckoo manager wants to fly off to the warmer climes and leave others to do the work.

Cuckoo managers are not selective in the work they delegate to others or to whom they delegate it. So long as they can dump their egg in someone else's nest, they don't really care. They 'lay lots of eggs' in the hope that some of them will be well tended and develop to maturity.

Many people have experienced the cuckoo manager. He indicates that he would like some new project investigated, but only has a vague notion of what is required. The subordinate then puts a lot of effort into the project and weeks later reports back to his boss, who now only had a vague recollection of what it was that he asked for, as his mind has moved on to something else. Those who have experienced this behaviour become wise to it after a while. They realize that the problem, project or opportunity dumped on them will probably be soon forgotten and so they put it to one side hoping that nothing more will come of it.

One of our clients once described a cuckoo manager to us, 'Only when she asks me to work on a new idea three times in a row will I commence it. In most cases she has forgotten about it because she has moved onto something new.'

Cuckoo managers don't seem to have the interest in taking their ideas and developing them to fruition. They prefer others to do it for them. However if the result does not align with their vision of the end product, they can be highly critical of the people carrying out the work. As one client said of a cuckoo manager, 'All he can do is look over our shoulder and tell us what is wrong. He never tells us what is right or gives us praise. He can't do it himself, but is ready to criticize everyone else.'

Sometimes cuckoo managers are described as the 'I' – 'We' – 'You' manager. When things are going well he says, 'That was a great idea I had.' When things are looking a little unsure he might say, 'We'll have to be a bit careful on this project.' When things are going badly, he is likely to say, 'You really made a mess of this project, didn't you.'

Tips for cuckoo managers

In the short term

- Explain to people what you want them to do and why.
- Formulate goals and outcomes together.
- Talk through the process of how the work might be carried out.
- Agree the parameters which will define whether the 'egg' has been well raised.
- Give praise continuously and recognize everyone's contribution to the work.

In the longer term

Try to develop your skills in analysis and following things through. It is easy to think up ideas and pass them to others to work on. It is much harder to carry out a rigorous filtering process to distinguish the good eggs from the bad.

Thought for the Cuckoo Manager

Dumping your problems on
others to repair
Fosters hostility, not unity
and care.

Chapter Ten

The Hedgehog

IT WAS THE BEST summer in five years. The lush, green hedgerows were full of birds and insects. Harry Hedgehog was happy; he loved the warm months almost as much as his winter sleep. He trundled around the hedgerows, burrowing his nose into the foliage to uncover his favourite morsels. This summer he would have to be more industrious than he wished, but he had a growing family and his wife needed help gathering food. Their youngsters were almost ready to leave home but he still needed to teach them how to forage for themselves. Soon though, he would be free to enjoy himself and snuffle around at his leisure.

There were many other males dwelling in Harry's field, but Harry was the most senior. He had lived in this part of the countryside all his life and knew every hedgerow, inside out. He considered himself to be the wisest and most talented hedgehog for miles around and became very upset if his friends suggested that he was wrong about a particular plant or insect. He would roll up into a ball and present his spines to them so they couldn't taunt him further.

As father, it was Harry's duty to teach his youngsters. Although full of good intentions, he was always too busy. There never seemed to be enough time for him to do what he wanted. His day seemed to pass so quickly in providing for his family and pursuing his own interests.

As senior hedgehog, it was Harry's duty to pass on his wisdom to the younger generation. However, again he could never find the time. When feasts occurred in the hedgerow it was Harry who had to find the delicacies, as he had never taught the other males where to look.

Now that Harry's offspring were ready to learn about the outside world, he set about the task of teaching them. He dearly wanted them to be independent so he could do the things he wanted to do. However, he was a poor teacher. He was very impatient with their faltering attempts at foraging and often became disgusted with them, making them stand aside so that he could do it himself. He sometimes wondered if he should bother at all, as it seemed quicker to just gather the food for them. 'Perhaps,' he thought, 'if I awoke a little earlier, I could see to their needs and then have the rest of the day for myself.'

The other hedgehogs laughed at him and said that if he didn't teach his offspring the ways of the hedgerow that they would be dependent upon him for the rest of his life and die when he did. Harry was furious and rolled into a ball so that the other hedgehogs would not interfere with him. He hated criticism. He would teach them all they needed, as soon as he had the time to show them. He thought that maybe if he waited another week or two they would be older and learn more quickly and then it wouldn't take so much time to show them.

His next attempt at education ended up with the same hesitant burrowing and feeble attempts at foraging by his pupils. Harry was now convinced that only he could do these tasks properly and so he started his day while it was still light and worked until after dawn.

The other hedgehogs were annoyed by Harry's attitude and found that their own offspring were copying Harry's, expecting the parents to do all the work. It was a potentially dangerous situation for the hedgehogs as relying on one family member to support the rest would limit their life expectancy. If the supporting member was killed on the road or died, then the family would struggle.

Harry was becoming very tired, as he found that all the extra work was just too much for him. He was so exhausted at the end of each day that he would just curl up and go to sleep without his dinner. His wife was worried about him and decided that it was time she stepped in and taught her offspring the ways of the hedgerow, before it was too late. The other hedgehogs were happy to help her and it wasn't long before the hedgerow was once again alive with hedgehogs snuffling and burrowing around the roots for food.

The expert

Ben Kramer was a perfectionist. Everyone in the office knew that any work that went through Ben's hands would be in perfect order, noted and filed. Ask Ben for a file and he always knew where to find it immediately. The file would be in chronological order and secured on file holders. Two minutes of reading would give the full picture of the contents, together with recommendations for outcomes.

Ben was so proud of his skills and became very upset if anyone dared criticize his methods. He had been in that job in the Social Security office for twenty years. He had declined any other positions offered as he loved his work. New governments had come and gone and new procedures had been requested, but in the twenty years he had been there, the job had altered very little. People still applied for the benefits offered and Ben was happy to check all the criteria in the applications against the current regulations. He was an expert and could find all the loopholes in the system and recognize those applications likely to be fraudulent. Colleagues described him as 'prickly' as he was likely to take offence if anyone suggested that he should improve the way things could be done.

The department considered Ben to be an asset, but they were a little disturbed by the long hours he put in as the work load increased. He never complained, as he enjoyed seeing the empty 'in' basket when he left at the end of the day. He hated anyone else touching his files as they didn't pay attention to details and he would have to redo the paperwork next time the file was used. It was much quicker and efficient to do it all himself, rather than relying on others who were likely to make mistakes.

Whenever Ben went on holiday, it caused problems, because no-one knew how to perform his job. Although his filing system was perfect and each file a masterpiece of efficiency, the procedures he went through to ensure that each application was legitimate were not documented; they were in Ben's head. Consequently Ben would return from holiday with an overflowing desk, but he was secretly pleased, as it underscored his value to the department.

Ben had great intentions of teaching others his methods of processing but he was just too busy to spare the time. He was afraid that if they didn't pick up the work very quickly, he would have to reprocess much of it himself. He often thought, 'By the time I teach them the work and then check that it has been done to my high standards, I might as well have done it myself!' He knew he really should make time to teach others, but it never seemed to get to the top of his priority list. After all, they were so slow and he would become impatient with their lack of knowledge.

There came the time when Ben felt he could never take holidays as the work piled up while he was away, and this, combined with the ever increasing daily applications, meant that he could never catch up. He was exhausted at the end of each day and his family were very concerned about him. He coped at work but almost collapsed when he came home. He was unable to sleep as he was concerned about the backlog of applications and the people waiting for his decisions to enable them to draw money to live. He would lay awake with his mind going round and round, as he attempted to find a solution to speed up his procedures without letting go of the accuracy.

His daughter decided that it was time for action and encouraged him to visit the doctor for some sleeping tablets to at least allow Ben a good night's sleep. Ben reluctantly went one Thursday evening during late surgery. The doctor told him that the state of his health was such that if he continued to work at this pace, he would end up being unable to work at all. The doctor insisted that Ben take time off work and rest. She prescribed various tablets and signed a certificate for sick leave. Ben's daughter ensured the tablets were taken as prescribed and the certificate went into the department, in case Ben once again decided that it was easier to just go to work!

Hedgehog managers

Hedgehog managers are hard-working people, usually with specialist knowledge. Often they have built up their knowledge over a number of years and have a reputation for being an expert. Consciously or unconsciously they have kept this knowledge to themselves and built it into a form of power. When colleagues challenge them or suggest that their behaviour may be impacting others, they 'roll into a ball' and become unapproachable. They take pride in their work and view advice as criticism.

Delegation is very difficult for hedgehog managers. Because of their focus on details and their high standards, they find it very hard to let go of work and give authority and responsibility to others. For them, the process of delegation is explaining to others how to do the work, then looking continuously over their shoulder to check that it is being done the right way, and finally double-checking the work before it moves to the next stage. Therefore, they say, 'It is quicker to do it myself.' Initially this may be the case but it is not long before long hours are being spent and stressful situations arise.

Hedgehog managers need to understand the process of delegation and the role of a teacher, a coach and a mentor. Delegation is not simply explaining to someone what needs to be done and then expecting perfection. It is a process which starts with learning and there must be both an individual and an organizational learning environment. Learning leads to competence, competence leads to confidence and confidence leads to trust. When this process is in place then organizations can function far more effectively.

To be an effective teacher, coach and mentor requires patience, understanding and commitment. Confidence in your own ability and a high self-esteem are also required so that you do not wield power through your expert knowledge.

Hedgehog managers also need to understand how people learn. A simple way of characterising this has been developed by Honey and Mumford (1982). They define four different learning styles as *activist, pragmatist, theorist* and *reflector. Activists* learn best by actually doing the task. They will make plenty of mistakes and therefore need a process which enables them to learn from these mistakes. If they receive criticism rather than advice to prevent it happening again, they will not learn effectively.

Pragmatist learners need to see the relevance of what they are learning to everyday practical outputs and outcomes. For them there must be a practical payoff for working in a particular way. *Reflectors* learn by watching, reflecting and then trying it on their own, with no one looking over their shoulder. *Theorists* need to understand how the work they are learning conceptually fits in with the 'big picture'. Therefore using different learning styles for different people can enhance the speed of learning.

Tips for hedgehog managers

In the short term

To avoid being a hedgehog manager:

- Accept that you are an expert in your area and that you don't have to continually prove yourself.
- When people criticize you, accept it as well-meaning advice.
- Remember that very few people on their death bed wished that they had spent more time at work. If you are spending long hours, ask yourself, 'who can help me?'
- Learn the process of delegation and accept that it takes time and considerable help in the form of coaching and counselling, before people can perform.

In the longer term

- Develop expertise as a teacher and a coach. Very few effective managers have these skills naturally. You will need to learn them.
- Continually review the work processes in your organization when people become overworked and stressed. Be open to new ideas and the advances in technology that can improve things.

Thought for the Hedgehog Manager

Practice makes perfect;
you know this is true.
Train and guide your staff so they
can learn to help you.

Chapter Eleven

The Weaverbird

IN SOUTHERN AFRICA the intricate and neat nests of the colourful weaverbirds hang from the trees growing in the veldts. Weaverbirds spend many hours collecting leaves and twigs for their nests, weaving them into an elliptical shape with a hole at the bottom for entry.

One such weaverbird lived in the Kruger National Park in the northern Transvaal. Living in a national park he was free from the threat of poachers and other unnatural predators, so his life was easy and relaxed.

Every spring, he would start to build a nest in the hope of attracting a new mate. Female weaverbirds are very fussy about the nest they choose to live in and can be very critical of the male's workmanship.

He set to work with his usual enthusiasm, as he enjoyed starting a new nest. It was a time for him to explore the countryside, looking for materials which would make the perfect nest. He would fly around for hours, eventually selecting only three pieces of grass or reed which he would meticulously weave into a perfect pattern. Hours later he would fly off again, searching for a few more ideal pieces of grass. He rarely spoke with the other weaverbirds, as he was too engrossed in his nest building.

Weaverbird nest building is a real work of art, but most other weaverbirds knew when to leave a nest. They would abandon the unfinished nest and the skeletal remains would disintegrate in the wind. They knew that some nests were just not worth finishing. Not so this weaverbird – he would stay with his nest whatever the problem.

Choosing a nest site is similar to choosing a house – you can never be certain of how it will feel until you live in it. This was his principle, so he would spend hours reinforcing one side of the nest where a rough twig poked its sharp finger into it each time the wind blew. He could not see that he was ignoring the main problem and just tinkering around the edges.

Some seasons, part of the nest would blow away but instead of realizing that it would be better to start again in a more sheltered spot he would repair the damage and continue to build.

The building of his nest took twice as long as the other weaverbirds. If a piece of grass would not bend just the right way, he would fiddle with it instead of dropping it and finding a more flexible piece. His nest had lots of stray ends poking out which he had unsuccessfully tried to mesh with the next piece. He decided to leave them until later to fix.

Interested females would fly around the nest and show him where it needed attention, but he would shoo them away, telling them to wait until it was finished before bothering him. Other males would bring him nesting materials that they had left over, but he rejected them, insisting on collecting his own materials.

As you can imagine, his nest was always rejected by the females because it had lots of loose ends that required finishing. By the time he had completed his work, placing the last strand over his fastidiously neat entrance, most of the females had already made their selection. It was always more by luck than good management that he got a mate at all! Only in the seasons when females were in abundance could he attract one of the 'left overs'. The natural need to reproduce the species would override the female's desire for a suitable home and so she would reluctantly accept the incomplete nest. She would put the finishing touches to the nest herself before the eggs were laid. In

this way she could be sure that it was safe and secure for her fledglings.

Every year he was undaunted and would set about his nest building in the same ambitious way, 'tinkering' with his selected materials until they met with his satisfaction. He never learnt to modify his ways because he didn't realize they needed changing. He liked to do things by himself and to his own plan, oblivious to those around him. He never noticed what others were doing and never really cared. He was satisfied with his own ability. The other male weaverbirds wanted to help him and give him advice, but he was very unapproachable and made it clear that he did not want to listen.

Nothing is urgent

Claudia Tyas was the office manager for a small firm of chartered accountants. Being a small firm, she was responsible, not only for the accounts, but also the general day-to-day running of the office. The partners in the firm travelled frequently and often worked from home. This left Claudia with a degree of autonomy to make her own administrative decisions.

Claudia was a very trustworthy person and loyal to the organization. She upheld the standards and ethics of the company and could be relied upon to ensure that all the accounts were settled on time and the employees' wages paid.

A new accounts system had been introduced which was separate from the financial package they used to monitor and service their customers. It was written with an accounting firm in mind and had many new features to make Claudia's life easier.

Claudia was thrilled and commenced learning the system immediately. Although she was efficient when dealing with areas she fully understood, time and deadlines had little impact on her when she faced a new challenge. She would spend hours reading the manual and 'tinkering' with the system to find out how to make certain commands in the program work. She had been offered a training course by the programmer of the package but she considered she knew enough about computers to teach herself from the manual.

This, of course, saved the company money in training, but it cost them dearly in time wasted trying to find out how a certain function worked. Instead of making a 'phone call to ask an expert for advice, she would spend hours attempting to sort out the problem herself. Occasionally she would find that the program had an error or was unable to produce the report she required. The programmers had offered a 'bespoke' service to customize the program to the organization's needs, but rather than contact them, Claudia would complain bitterly to everyone, sighing heavily. Had the programmer been telephoned, the problem could have been fixed with the minimum of fuss. Claudia did not trust the computer package and so she also kept her own set of manual accounts which recorded all the details in a meticulous manner.

The partners would put in their expense forms for reimbursement and rely on Claudia to arrange payment. Claudia would deal with these when she considered it was appropriate and sometimes weeks would go by before payment was received. Sometimes the partners felt that they were asking for Claudia's own money rather than the company's. If the partners needed a cheque or a report, they would often set a date by which it was required. Usually this date was two weeks before they really needed it, to allow for what they called 'the Claudia factor'.

The rest of the staff were also wary of Claudia and dreaded asking for an amended invoice or even worse, cancelling one. Some staff members paid for things out of their own pockets rather than ask her for reimbursement. Everything appeared to be a bother to her and any requests were treated as interference. She never seemed to have enough time in the day to do her job and even the simplest tasks took a long time.

The stationery supplies were often a contentious issue as requesting more stationery was subject to the same attitude as invoicing. Claudia was very careful with the supplies and never over-ordered in case the staff might waste them. Sometimes customer mail outs were delayed because stationery supplies were low and no one was brave enough to approach Claudia. They preferred to wait for the next routine order. Only the boldest of staff would request an urgent order!

Claudia was a very private person and never revealed much about her out-of-work activities. She was always willing to join in the staff functions and was very pleasant once she had had her first glass of wine. In the office, however, she seemed to have the world on her shoulders and was rarely cheerful. When she arrived at work people could almost sense the negative energy field around her, which soon enveloped the work space and affected everyone. Sometimes she would chat for a while but would soon return to her office to study her computer manuals or devise a new recording system for monitoring daily telephone calls.

Weaverbird managers

Weaverbird managers are often quieter people who prefer to work on their own or in small groups. They set high personal standards and like to keep working on a task until they get it finished. Each part of the project must be completed to their satisfaction before they move onto the next part. They tend to be oblivious to time constraints and nothing is ever urgent. People and projects can wait until the 'weaverbird' is ready to deal with the issues!

Weaverbird managers seem to love acquiring information which they like to keep to themselves. Even if they don't fully understand the information they have, they will still spend hours experimenting with it until they can make it work. In most cases the task or project could be completed in half the time if only the weaverbird manager realized that she had a team around her to help and experts in the outside world to give advice.

There are many pressures on managers today. They have multiple responsibilities and are expected to do 'more with less'. There simply is not time available to spend worrying, experimenting or 'tinkering' until a solution is found. If the solution is not immediately obvious then others should be consulted as quickly as possible.

If you tend to be a weaverbird, yourself, then it is essential for you to implement a system of time management. A manager's time needs to be balanced between analysing information and implementing action. Weaverbirds spend too much time on experimenting or 'tinkering', and not enough time on action.

Tips for weaverbird managers

In the short term

You can improve your performance by using a time planner and regularly monitoring your outputs.

- Try listing the tasks you have to accomplish, with realistic dates for completion. Review each week whether you are on target.
- When faced with a new task ask yourself if you have the skills to do it. If you don't, then consider whether there is time to learn these skills or whether it is better to delegate this work to someone else.
- Review each day whether your quest for perfection is causing delivery dates to be delayed. If so, then ask yourself, 'who can help me?' Telephone an expert or ask the advice of someone in your organization.
- Make sure that you can distinguish the important task from the urgent one. To many weaverbirds, the urgent matters are those they are interested in. The important issues are often put to one side. To help you differentiate between the two, try asking the question, 'what would happen if I didn't do this today?' In this way the list of important things to do should become clearer.

In the longer term

Try to develop a far more action-oriented way of working. Organizations appreciate managers who can make things happen. Not everything has to be 100 per cent perfect before getting into action! Select a task that you do on a regular basis and then work out how you could complete it in 20 per cent less time.

Thought for the Weaverbird Manager

Why waste time on tasks where your competence is low? Demonstrate your skills in areas that you know.

Chapter Twelve

The Peacock

THE ELDER-PEACOCK was very proud of himself. He strutted about the place, pecking here and there and showing off his wonderful plumage.

The Elder-Peacock was very vain and was constantly preening himself to make sure he looked at his best. His partner, the Elder-Peahen, was in awe of him and saw to his every need. She constantly told him how wonderful he was, which was just what he wanted to hear.

The rest of the peacock community disliked his vanity and avoided him whenever possible. As elder peacock, he liked to regularly visit everyone and make sure that their homes were tidy and that the community was keeping the standards that he liked.

He would poke around in their nests looking for stray twigs and feathers which he would point out with relish, telling them how lucky they were to have such a caring elder. He was never known to praise a tidy nest, only criticize an unkempt one.

As he was the elder in the community, he thought that his plumage was the only one worth showing. If any of the younger peacocks tried to show their feathers, he would immediately chase them away. He would then spread his magnificent tail in triumph.

As the seasons passed, his plumage became bedraggled and

many of his feathers no longer grew so long and strong. His vanity prevented his noticing their bedraggled appearance. He refused to look at himself and as the Elder-Peahen still told him he was handsome, he ignored the community.

He continued to check all the nests and became more and more meticulous in his searches. He upset everyone and the community felt that they were not allowed any freedom to live their own lives. Their morale declined and many of them just sat on their nests all day, to avoid the interference of the Elder-Peacock.

There were many challenges for the elder's position but, despite his age and deteriorating plumage, he managed to ward off defeat. The younger peacocks felt guilty but realized that the elder's power would eventually decline like his feathers, and they must bide their time. Sooner or later their turn would come and they vowed never to be like the Elder-Peacock. Meanwhile their task was to hold the community together awaiting the better times that would surely come.

High ego

John Jackson was the director of a small mail order business with a staff of fifteen people. He was very outgoing and enthusiastic and strongly believed in his own capabilities. He had started the business with a colleague some five years ago but lacked management ability and strongly relied on his partner for the growth of the business. Staff would often jokingly say that John and his wife were in love with the same man!

John was happiest when he was working with ideas, considering what new directions the business should take. However, most of his ideas were impractical and his partner would often describe them as 'whacky'.

When interacting with staff, John would never praise any ideas that came from other people. Bev, the promotions manager, called him 'yes-but John' because when presented with a new idea, John would immediately proceed to point out why the idea would not work. However, if anyone criticized John's ideas he would be offended and look to ways of 'getting his own back'.

After work finished for the day, John would snoop around every-one's desk rifling their drawers to see what they had been doing. He had learned this technique earlier in his career when he had 'acquired' the key to his boss's filing cabinet and would come in over the weekend to get valuable 'ammunition' which he would often use against his boss. John thought that nobody realized what he was doing, but the practice was widely known and some of the more mischievous staff left 'red herrings' for John to find.

John was not a good copy writer but could not resist changing the promotional campaigns thought up by Bev. Often Bev would have a first sketch and early storyboard for a campaign lying on her desk. Overnight, John would go through her work and leave messages all over the draft, explaining what was wrong with it.

John's actions succeeded in undermining the spirit of the team and over a period of time the morale slipped drastically. People started coming to work late and leaving early. For many of the staff, working in the company was just a job and their real life commenced after 5:00pm or at weekends.

When John delegated tasks to the staff he would explain in very vague terms what was required and then criticize people when they failed to deliver what he specifically wanted.

Susan, the finance manager of the company, was a tireless worker and took pride in her reputation for honesty and diligence. She was a signatory to the main cheque account along with the promotions manager, although either director could sign as well. This arrangement had been in place for the five years that Susan had been with the company. One day John came in to Susan and said that he wanted to change the banking arrangements by setting a limit of $10,000 on any cheques that Susan signed. Amounts in excess of this would need both directors' signatures. Susan had regularly signed for amounts in excess of $50,000 as both directors travelled regularly and were often out of town. When asked why this action was required, John jokingly said it was to stop Susan running off to Brazil with the company's assets.

Two weeks later Susan resigned from the company along with Bev and two others. John immediately departed overseas on a business trip and left his partner to sort out the mess, claiming that his partner was upsetting the staff and causing them to leave.

Peacock managers

Many managers we have worked with allow their egos to interfere with their abilities. When appointed to a senior position they try to use the power of the position to drive home their wishes, rather than trying to empower the team to steer itself towards the organizational goals.

It is a wise person who knows her weaknesses. Unfortunately people with high egos will not accept that they have weaknesses and carry with them an 'illusion of invulnerability'. John Jackson had a great ability to promote the work of the business and interact externally with key stakeholders such as customers. He considered this to be the 'real' work of the business and devalued all the efforts put in by his staff in the areas of marketing, administration and accounts. He had no knowledge of the procedures involved in these areas and his authoritative manner indicated to everyone that he knew better than they did. His actions indicated that he did not trust them to do a good job.

A measure of humility would have enabled John to be far more effective as a manager. In western society there seems to be an unwritten law that if you are in a position of authority, then you know more than your subordinates. Nothing could be further from the truth. What John needed to do was set the vision and the goals for his team and then let them get on and deliver the excellence he required. A way to start this is through self-discovery by recognizing what you are good at and what you should leave to others. Treating others professionally and respecting them for their abilities and personal characteristics is the foundation of good leadership.

Many peacock managers will delegate work to others and then expect them to deliver results. However, unless people have the skills to carry out a job then they will predictably fail to deliver work of the right standard. This invariably encourages the peacock to punish them by 'poking his nose into their business', checking and double checking their work, telling them what is wrong rather than developing them to do what is right.

The journey to trust starts with defining roles and responsibilities and delegating tasks to be performed against agreed standards. This invariably requires considerable training and development, coaching, and mentoring, which leads to competence to carry out the job. This, then, leads to confidence which in turn will put the wheels of 'trust' into motion. However, this process can take a long time, which is why few managers seem to do it. If only the TRUTH fairy were real!

Tips for peacock managers

In the short term

- Don't micro-manage the work of your team.
- Practise humility.
- Regard mistakes as a learning experience.
- Set the goals and the vision and then let people deliver them in their own way.

In the longer term

- Understand your strengths and weaknesses and those of the people around you.
- Seek feedback from your staff and be prepared to change.
- Make sure that you have training mechanisms in place.

Thought for the Peacock Manager

*If you think all around you are
incompetent and slow,
Make sure the problem is not the
size of your ego!*

Chapter Thirteen

The Kookaburra

THERE IS A HIERARCHY in every community, even in the Australian bush. The natural leaders are the kookaburras who perch high in the trees watching everything that moves. The kookaburra makes a long, loud, laughing sound indicating that it must surely be an animal that enjoys having fun.

In one part of the outback bush, lived Kevin Kookaburra. He spent most of the time high in his tree watching for the slightest movement on the forest floor. Then he would swoop down to devour a tasty witchetty grub. As chief kookaburra in this region, he was often consulted for his advice, but he just wanted to have fun all day and laugh out loud.

When there was a party or games to be played, Kevin was always there. When there was work to be done, he was noticeably absent, snoozing on his high perch. The bush community began to lose their respect for him. How could they trust his judgement when he didn't care when there was a problem? How could he solve their problems when he only wanted to share the fun?

Kevin's behaviour caused the forest to become restless. Many of the creatures in the forest started to change their behaviour too.

The mischievous imps decided they didn't want to help with the work either. What was good enough for the kookaburra, was good enough for them. So they spent all their time playing tricks on everyone. The fairies were frightened by this new turn of events and kept to their part of the bush. They did not venture out unless it was necessary. The goannas began to steal the emus' eggs and the wallabies roamed the forest, eating anything that took their fancy. They particularly liked the carefully-kept gardens of the fairies and the vegetable patches of the elves. The forest became untidy as no-one tended it. Everyone was more interested in looking after themselves than caring about others.

The community spirit deteriorated and no-one but the imps had fun. Kevin joined in many of their pranks but there seemed to be more and more problems arising and much less fun to be had. Kevin now spent much of his time away from his perch as he was constantly beseeched by the forest inhabitants to do something to solve the community problems. It all seemed like too much hard work for him, so he flew off when he saw them approaching.

The elves decided that they should be the ones to repair the forest before it deteriorated further. None of the other creatures seemed to care about their community; they were busy tending to their own needs. The fairies were concerned and wanted to help but were afraid of conflict. The Fairy Queen was pleased when at last the elves began to rescue the situation.

The chief elf was very wise and knew exactly what to do – nothing! The kookaburra had to set an example for the community but Kevin was unprepared to do so. If they waited a while, he would tire of the situation and fly off to a new part of the bush.

So the elves let the forest deteriorate a little further, until the community stopped dancing and ceased playing. Kevin, as predicted, became very bored. There was no longer anything to laugh about. Each day he ventured further away looking for excitement elsewhere. One day he failed to return. He had found another community to live where he could laugh and have fun.

The elves were overjoyed and began looking for a replacement leader. The chief elf approached the Kookaburra Council and explained the problem. One of the councillors came himself, to set an example of what a kookaburra should do. Of course they had to laugh and have fun, but only if they worked hard!

It didn't take long for the forest to become the place it had once been where everyone was kind, caring and helpful. The gardens blossomed and the dancing resumed. Eventually a new kookaburra was selected as permanent leader and set up residence. He was reliable and trustworthy.

Too much fun

The toy factory was the pride of the small village, producing unique toys and employing most of the villagers. Each year production increased as their toys became more popular. Soon it was a status symbol for children to own toys from the village. An annual festival was arranged on the theme of 'Toyland' and thousands of people would arrive to show their children the home of their famous toys.

The old factory manager eventually retired and a new younger manager replaced him. Vernon Mpofu had graduated from university with first class honours in business studies and then continued on as a post-graduate MBA student. He had been voted as the student most likely to succeed. He had an outgoing personality and was very popular with his peers. The toy factory was delighted when he decided to join them. He had been at university for eight years and knew all the business theory there was to know. He was enthusiastic and couldn't wait to get started.

During the management transition, he decided that the way to learn about the factory was to work for a time in every department. He thoroughly enjoyed learning about the business and particularly liked joining the staff on their drinks evening, each Friday. Everybody liked him as he was happy to 'get his hands dirty' by working on the shop floor. He was soon able to get to know everybody and fully understand the toy-making processes. When he took over completely from the old manager, he found that his day was occupied with planning and decision making, which he found very boring. He wanted to be out 'managing by wandering around', interacting with all the staff who had got to know him quite well. So he made sure that a large part of his day was spent interacting with the workers.

The staff initially enjoyed his involvement with their work but soon relationships began to sour. Although Vernon spent time talking with others, it was often on peripheral issues. He began to lose their respect as he rarely solved their problems, and spent too much time talking, rather than acting. He was rarely in his office to receive phone calls and the administration staff could never find him. All they knew was that he was somewhere in the factory. The factory lost its efficiency and direction as Vernon failed to set an example for others to follow.

Some of the shop floor workers decided to take longer tea breaks and would often play cards when they were supposed to be working. Friday afternoons were no longer spent at work; they would finish at lunch time and spend the afternoon in the bar. Vernon would sometimes be with them. The office staff were very worried about this as they could see at first hand that orders were being filled late and only their reputation was keeping the customers.

The supervisors were having difficulty keeping discipline because, as often as not, Vernon was with the workers. It was difficult to demand their return to work when the manager condoned it. Vernon really thought he was doing a great job and that people liked his relaxed, friendly management style. He had to admit though, that he was becoming bored. He knew the toy business now and it was no longer a challenge. Going to the bar wasn't nearly so much fun these days either, as the conversation wasn't stimulating and he had heard all their jokes before.

He started to look around for another position which would excite his interest again. It was time to gain experience in another industry where he could use his ability and wits. Maybe merchant banking or stockbroking would suit him better than the mundane activities of toy making. He soon talked his way into a new job in the city and left. There was a big farewell party for him and many of the staff breathed a sigh of relief. They were not sad to see him go. With the right replacement they may just be able to prevent the factory from ruin.

Kookaburra managers

Leaders act as a 'role model' for staff. People look to their managers, not just as a source of authority, but as individuals who earn respect through the behaviour they model. Managers should recognize that they set an example in everything that they do – from the quick off-the-cuff remark to the processes they use with colleagues. Staff take their cues from the leader as to what is expected and acceptable. The

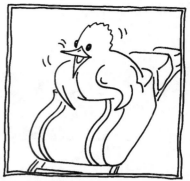

manager who continually arrives at work after the other members of his team, and then leaves on the dot of five o'clock, cannot be surprised if his staff are unwilling to burn the midnight oil.

As with most things, being a role model is a question of balance. Vernon had the right ideas of 'managing by wandering around' and being close to his workers, but he tipped the balance the wrong way. There is no doubt that having fun is an important part of work. Playing and working (plorking) definitely lead to increased motivation but most people find getting the right balance difficult. Popular proverbs like 'All work and no play make Jackie a dull boy' and 'Running with the hares and hunting with the hounds' attest to the problems many people have faced down the ages. In our experience, people who are committed to work, but also have strong outside interests, have developed a psychic balance that contributes to excellence in their lives.

Leaders who are 'workaholics' create problems for their staff. This is setting a negative example. A leader who regularly telephones staff at home outside working hours or who expects people to continually work late is setting an example which can actually decrease the morale and motivation of the team. These leaders often expect their team members to be as committed as them, devoting every waking hour to thinking about the organization.

Kookaburra managers are 'laissez-faire' managers. Their organization usually has enough momentum of its own to keep going and they are merely passengers riding on the roller-coaster. They could substantially influence the direction of the organization but only if they combine their skills and interest in people with a focus on a direction for their business.

Tips for kookaburra managers

In the short term

- Mark your style as a leader on the work-play continuum:

    Work_____Play

    Is the balance right for you?

- Think of ways to 'plork'. This involves creating 'play' situations which are focused on business objectives.
- List the standards you expect of your staff. Are your expectations too high? Are you a workaholic?

In the longer term

Try to develop a vision for your organization. You can do this by involving your staff and having fun at the same time. Ensure that the values of 'pleasure' are incorporated in your vision, but make sure that the goals and objectives will challenge and stretch your staff.

Thought for the Kookaburra Manager

Fun must be part of the working day,
as the hours are long;
Learning to balance hard work and
play will make your team strong.

Part Three

Team Stories

Some teams perform like a well-oiled machine, whereas others fall into disrepair. In this section of the book we have crafted team stories from animals which work in teams and likened them to problems we have encountered in organizations today.

The animal team stories use a mixture of natural lifestyles and enforced lifestyles to describe common problems that occur when animals work in teams. The behaviour we have observed in these animals is very similar to that of humans trying to collaborate in work groups.

The team stories came from problems with teamwork that we have encountered over the last few years. These take the format of a case study and highlight real problems in leadership. They can be used as a way of getting teams to review their own performance. Choosing an appropriate story to discuss at a team meeting can be a powerful way of initiating change.

The last part of each story contains our recommendations for improving teamwork. The themes cover strategic thinking, team management, values and team breakdown. Each of these topics almost requires a book on its own! We have tried to distil the essential ingredients into a few lines of advice.

The two styles of stories in each chapter reflect the same problems and are designed to present similar ideas in different formats. They can be enjoyed as an individual read or presented on training workshops as a way of initiating discussion on key elements of teamwork.

Chapter Fourteen

Beavers

BEAVERS ARE INDUSTRIOUS creatures, being undaunted by hard work. Their habitat is the river and its bank, and their lives are continually governed by floods and droughts. Survival depends upon their resolve to duty.

The rivers of North America are full of beavers. In one such river there lived many families whose territories had been established over several generations. Each adolescent male would seek out a new reach nearby and establish his home, hoping to attract a mate.

The families coexisted happily, each living separate lives. They were unaware of one another's daily activities, nor did they care. They kept to themselves, ensuring that their own section of river was as comfortable as they could make it. Daily, they gnawed at saplings and felled them, building and repairing the dam to create a deeper pond in which to live. Diligently they plugged the gaps in the dam wall, stemming the water flow to create a peaceful environment for their young. A deeper pond would increase their food supply.

Each family's world was confined to their part of the river. For them, nothing existed beyond. Otherwise they would be encroaching on the habitat of a relative. However, the families were not independent. The actions of one colony impacted another. Viewed from above it was easy to see how the hundreds of beaver colonies were affecting the flow of the river. It was developing a new course as dammed water flowed across the flat plains into virgin areas.

Oblivious to the impact of their natural instincts, the families 'beavered away', building and maintaining their dams. They could not see the 'big picture'. The practical results of their efforts focused on providing food and shelter only for themselves.

Often, a family moving in upstream would build a new dam, causing a downstream family to lose water and therefore look for a new home. The impact cascaded down the river as each colony reacted to the changed circumstances. Nobody ever bothered to ask the question, 'why?' Their instinct for survival was paramount in their minds.

Every year, during the wet season, heavy rains fell. Each beaver family would reinforce the dam to provide extra protection. Whenever the water level rose, they would build the dam wall a little higher, thereby retaining more and more water. When the floods came, every three years or so, the water pressure was too great and the dam walls broke, releasing a gush of water. Like dominos, the walls fell as the water rushed downstream.

Each breaking wall magnified the effect, increasing the thrust of the water as it gained momentum. Some beavers survived but many lost their homes and their young. In the lower reaches of the valley, the river burst its banks, flooding a nearby village and drowning animals and children in its wake.

Grinding to a halt

In the mountainous area of Kenya there are many coffee plantations and processing factories. Kenyan coffee is famous throughout the world for its unique flavour.

In one of these factories, coffee had been processed for generations, ownership passing frequently from person to person. The various owners had concentrated their efforts on marketing the product and the current owner was a member of the Kenyian marketing board. The factory supervisors were left to run the operation and ensure that high quality coffee was regularly produced.

Over the years there had been little change in the methods used to process coffee, apart from the addition of a decaffination section to meet new market tastes. Each department dealt with one aspect of coffee production and neither knew nor cared what happened to the product once it left their section.

One supervisor organized the picking of the beans. He had a small workforce that kept the factory going, but supply was a problem when heavy rain fell. The grinding and roasting section had variable output depending on the bean variety and the soil type. The decaffination section used only one type of bean and the freeze drier operation depended on the supply of bottles from the bottling plant.

The supervisors never had meetings and the only time they communicated was when one section was slow in processing, causing delays in a 'downstream' section. This effect would pass through the plant, causing disruptions to the instant and decaffinated coffee outputs. It was only after the problems occurred that action was taken. This often meant that the next section in the process line could be held up or overloaded with work. Consequently, production flow was inconsistent; when some sections needed overtime, others were laying off their workers.

The supervisors had their own way of working and would implement changes to their section without consulting the other supervisors. Their focus was on improving their part of the factory, regardless of the other sections' activities. The owner was too busy with marketing and rarely visited the factory to communicate face-to-face. He simply sent memos demanding increases in production to meet overseas orders.

In the meantime, the coffee was being marketed to the world in expensive television and newspaper advertising campaigns. Images of quality and reliability promoted the superiority of Kenyan coffee. The advertising was highly successful and the orders increased daily. The owner was delighted and signed contracts which doubled his sales. He asked the factory to increase production to match sales, but discovered, to his dismay, that their outdated machinery in older parts of the plant could not deliver high quality coffee, when pushed to their limits. Their newly-won customers soon tired of the late, poor-quality coffee delivered to them. In no way did it match the promise of the slick advertising campaign.

Word soon got around the coffee buyers and sales plummetted. In a very short time the factory had to close and all the workers were made redundant, leaving behind a pile of unfilled orders and outdated machinery.

Strategic thinking

So many organizations today are like beaver colonies. Each section or department gets on with its own business and no attempt is made to see the big picture. How often do we hear the words 'them' and 'us' uttered to describe sections of an organization? It is almost as if the different parts of the organization are in competition with one another, rather than pulling in the same direction. To some extent, the structure of organizations into various departments, each performing a specific function, has contributed to this. Accountants, engineers and marketeers all speak a different language and like the beavers will go out of their way to protect their territory, rather than seeing how they can cooperate for the benefit of the whole organization.

No section, branch or department can work in isolation. Organizations are systemic, part of a huge cybernetic system where outputs from one part become inputs to another. The challenge of modern management is to see this big picture and to understand the interactions of all the key elements comprising an organization. The external environment is changing at such a rapid rate that we must continually monitor every aspect of work and adapt, so that the overall outcomes of the organization are enhanced by the outputs of the individual parts.

The key to success in any cybernetic system is flexibility. The first law of cybernetics states that in anything that operates systemically, the elements of the system that have the greatest flexibility or adaptability are the ones that gain control. This law is sometimes known as the Law of Requisite Variety. It is the governing law for survival in nature where the organic species that adapt to changes are the ones that survive.

In business, survival also depends on adaptability which is only possible by thinking strategically – by seeing the 'big picture'. It requires you to stand back from the cut and thrust of daily life and examine the purpose of what you are doing. How do all the parts of the business interact to achieve the grand plan? What impact will external environmental issues have on my organization? How can I plan to avoid a catastrophe?

For many people it is difficult to 'zoom out' and see the

relationships between individual parts. Like the beavers, they work in their own 'box', never bothering to open the lid and admire the beauty and excitement of what lies beyond. It requires skill, experience and determination to do this.

In the *Fifth Discipline Fieldbook* (Senge *et al.*, 1994), the authors describe the importance of systems thinking in a learning organization. The concepts are based upon the techniques of systems dynamics which analyse how complex feedback processes can generate problematic patterns of behaviour within organizations and large-scale human systems. They present several systems archetypes which show how the best solutions are often those which are unrelated in time and space to the presenting problem.

Of particular interest is the 'shifting the burden' archetype which differentiates between the 'quick fix' and the underlying root cause of a problem. A good example from everyday life is the headache. The quick fix is an aspirin but this doesn't solve the long-term problem which could be any one of a number of defects in other parts of the body. A strategic thinker will spend time looking for the root cause whereas many people would simply opt for the obvious solution of 'more aspirin, more often'.

Tips to improve strategic thinking

In the short term

- Draw up a box representing your section, branch, department or organization.
- List the inputs required for your box to work.
- Now list the outputs you create and where they go.
- How is your box affected by variations in the input?
- How is your box affected by variations in the output?

In the longer term

- Try to develop skills in scenario planning. Imagine all the possibilities that might occur in the future and how they might impact upon your work.
- Experiment with the processes of *systemic thinking* or *future mapping* (Phillips, 1996) which help project you into the future so that you can see how you may have to adapt in order to survive.

Chapter Fifteen

Huskies

I̲T WAS BITTERLY COLD and the arctic winds blew mercilessly across the vast icy expanse. The team of huskies lay huddled together for warmth behind a snow drift which sheltered them from the worst of the blasting winds. Their human team was camped in a tent behind a nearby cliff. It was an eerie, cold, pitch-black night with a bright canopy of stars covering this remote and unfriendly land.

As morning broke, the temperature remained low; the weak sun did not warm this area of frozen earth. Life was hard in this harsh climate, a mistake by one could cause the death of many. The husky team were as aware of this as the humans. The reward for their effort was a nutritious, fatty meal which kept up their resistance to the cold. They were adapted to the low temperatures, but relied on the humans totally for food. They trusted their handlers as they had been trained to expect food for work.

As the sun rushed above the horizon, the pulsating sounds of an engine could be heard. A large helicopter rounded the headland and slowly descended onto the frozen terrain. Three men scrambled from their tent and climbed into the cabin. The rotor blade whipped up the snow, causing the huskies to bark and strain at their leashes. It was a terrifying experience for them.

Unbeknown to the huskies, the leader of the human team was suffering severe frost bite. They had decided to abandon the expedition until all three could continue. Their plan was to be airlifted to the base camp and to send a dog handler back to feed the huskies and guide them home. Neither of the two remaining team members was willing to remain with the dogs.

The huskies were unable to comprehend this action. The people who fed them and looked after them were now gone. Feelings of abandonment and desperation welled within them. Tethered and hungry, they barked and struggled with the ropes restraining them. It took a great deal of effort to slip their leashes, but eventually they gained their freedom. Some were still joined together but they were free to move around.

The huskies ransacked the camp, eating anything they could find in the small tent. They turned on each other as they fought hard over the morsels. Instinct told them to head for base camp and so they scattered, running blindly over the frozen, barren wasteland in worsening weather. Tracks were impossible to follow in this snowy desert. They were lost and helpless.

Some of the huskies returned to the camp, fearful of the unknown. Others continued on but were never seen again. The wounded died very quickly, succumbing to the bitter, cold blizzard. Their carcasses were food for the few huskies who remained in the vicinity of the camp.

When the dog handler arrived at the camp, just four days later, he found only three dogs from the team of twelve huskies. They were in poor condition and extremely aggressive from their ordeal. The dog handler knew that the dogs didn't have the strength or the will to pull the sled to base camp. Their trust had been destroyed forever.

Lack of support

The production team in an video manufacturing company were making great progress in their team-building efforts. They were developing a self-directed team and had attended several workshops on personal understanding and group dependence.

Many of them had interesting hobbies which gave them the challenge and stimulation in life to cope with fairly routine work. Producing the cases for video cassettes was an important task for the company but the production itself was simple and structured. The team had devised systems and procedures which made the production much faster and ensured consistent quality. They prided themselves on the huge pile of perfect cases they stacked in the store room each day.

The company encouraged their team-building activities. The managers did not participate themselves, but they knew what was happening and read the reports with interest. They had little contact with the team, apart from infrequent visits to the shop floor and the exchange of memos requesting information or advising of new products.

Although the work environment was not ideal, the team was committed, as they had built up high levels of respect, understanding and trust. This confidence in their own ability gave them the ambition to succeed and the lack of information from the managers was seen as 'no news is good news'.

The managers often mentioned the success of the production team in their monthly reports to the directors. The efficiency of the team was outstanding and they took pride in the results they achieved. They were sure that if their work was unsatisfactory, then they would hear of it. So it was hardly surprising that the team was devastated when they read in the morning newspaper that the video case production unit was being closed down, as it was no longer viable.

The company had found that they could save money by importing the video cases from Taiwan. The cases were not quite as good as their own manufactured ones but quite adequate for the videos they produced. The company had been investigating the possibility of importing the cases for quite a while and had accepted a tender from Taiwan, as it was much cheaper than they had estimated. They had to accept within seven days to guarantee delivery.

The team could not believe that this proposed closure had never been mentioned to them. They had put hours of effort into their part of the company and as far as they knew, they were highly regarded by the directors.

Team members quickly 'phoned one another at home, the moment they read about it in the newspaper. A few only found out when they arrived at the factory. Some team members just turned around and went home, too shocked to comprehend that their jobs were lost and the factory would close. Others were indignant and tried to meet with the managers; others just sat at their still machinery and contemplated the grim future without income.

Values hierarchy

One of the basic human values that is that the foundation stone of all relationships is 'trust'. Without trust there can be no teamwork.

Personal values are the ideals that give significance to our lives and are usually expressed by principles that govern our priorities. There would be very few people not espousing that 'trust' is in the top section of their values hierarchy.

However, there is often a difference between what is 'espoused' and what is carried out in practice. In addition, the interpretation of 'trust' will actually depend on other values held in an individual's hierarchy. You might, for example, give someone information in confidence and then trust them not to tell others. However, if the information you give triggers off a value of 'ethics' or 'fairness' which is held at a higher level than 'confidentiality' then the other person may ignore your request for confidence as these higher order values 'switch in' and govern their action.

So it is not so much the individual values that a person or organization has, but more a combination of values that impact upon levels of trust. These combinations determine whether or not choices lead to creative, life-giving ends or destructive ones. For example, if a manager has a value of *customer service* combined with one of *productivity* one could expect a behaviour that would be respected and valued by the organization and its employees. However if the value of *competition* was equally important in the person's values hierarchy and

this was expressed in his or her relationship with peers, it might result in a lack of trust with resulting negative consequences.

In the work place there are a few basic values which need to be shared by leaders, staff and the business owners or organizational stakeholders, if foundations of trust are to be laid. These are *openness, honesty, integrity* and *commitment.*

Openness means being willing to indicate your views on situations, rather than bottling up your feelings and then talking about others behind their back or indulging in hidden agendas. However, like all values, they can be taken to extremes if you are not careful. Too much openness may lead to tactless interactions and this can have a negative impact on motivation. Too little openness and you will be accused of all sorts of things, as rumours ripple around the organization.

The ancient Greek philosopher Diogenes is said to have searched the streets of Athens with a lantern, looking for an honest person. Diogenes founded the school of philosophy known as the Cynics, so one can assume that he was unsuccessful! *Honesty* is one of the 'motherhood' values and one that everyone espouses. However, honesty is relative to your values hierarchy and what is honest to one person can be dishonest to another. Honesty in the work environment is all about telling things the way they are, rather than deceiving, manipulating or camouflaging hidden agendas.

Integrity is about 'wholeness' and consistency. Integrity is the regular application of your values hierarchy so that your behaviour is consistent in all situations. Whether you agree or disagree with someone, when they exhibit integrity, you will always know where they stand because they exhibit constancy in their dealings.

Commitment is a two-way street. When work is assigned to someone to be delivered to an agreed standard and a set date, a manager has the right to expect the person to be committed to the task and to complete it as planned. If problems arise, then openness becomes important to ensure that there is a free exchange of information. This then allows mistakes to be discussed and rectified in a learning environment. With such a process, the manager 'trusts' the other person to deliver the results. In return, employees should expect managers to be committed to supporting and developing them to give of their best in accordance with their ability.

In the video company case, there was no openness and one could argue that management was dishonest in not informing the workers of the negotiations taking place. They may have been able to justify secrecy in the early stages of negotiations but there comes a stage when openness and honesty are essential. In this case the management argued that people would leave and look for other jobs if they knew there was a possibility of the company being closed. Hence they justified their secrecy. However, it is our experience that once a culture of trust is established, then such situations are less likely to occur.

Tips for reviewing values

In the short term

■ Consider to what extent you value *trust* as a personal quality. Do this by listing the five most important values that drive you as a human being. Now insert the values of *trust, openness, honesty, integrity* and *commitment* into this list, in order of importance. Which of your values are more important than these and how does the combination drive your behaviour?

■ Develop an action plan on how you will increase the level of trust in your team/organization and the processes you will implement to ensure greater openness, honesty, integrity and commitment.

In the longer term

Carry out an analysis of the shared values within your organization. Some of the greatest conflicts occur in an organization when the values hierarchy of individuals is different.

Chapter Sixteen

Horses

R AIF CLEMENTS RAN a coaching house providing teams of horses for stage coaches on the mail run from North to South Dakota. Raif's horse teams were all different. Some worked really well together, but others failed to cooperate.

Raif spent hours trying to understand his horses and experimented with all sorts of combinations. His aim was to form the right groupings so that each team was a high-performing one. But some teams just never seemed to work well. He tried mixing up his teams, but this spoiled the good teams and made the poor teams no better. He found it very frustrating and often considered selling the troublesome teams and buying fresh horses. But many had been at his stables for years, and he was attached to them, despite all their idiosyncrasies.

His first class team, which he hired out to customers at a premium rate, were of no different pedigree to the rest of the stable. All his horses were strong and well fed, but those in his top team had something about them that was different. Although they had distinct personalities, they liked and respected one another. Out of harness, they played and ran together in the exercise yards. They pranced up and down the corral, playfully nipping and nuzzling each other. In harness, they were a team. The lead horses knew their work well and would encourage the rest of the team to keep on track and maintain a good speed. The team was very popular with the customers who were happy to pay the higher rate for a superior team, which ensured that the coach arrived on time at its destination.

The next team was a lively set of horses. They loved the run and were always eager to be harnessed. It was almost as if they lived for their work. They knew that when the stage coach arrived that it would be their job to pull it to the next stables. After a day's rest they would return to their own base. At the first distant rumble they would prick their ears. The billowing dust clouds told them it would only be an hour or so before they were on their way. They became restless in anticipation of some exercise. The passengers were often generous with sugar and apples and this made them even more impatient to get under way.

The difference between this team and the first team was the way they interacted when work was over for the day. These horses preferred to be alone, rarely seeking each other's company as they grazed the fields. The horses were similar in many ways, all preferring solitary time while their bodies recharged with energy for the next journey. When they were linked together in harness, they were as good as the first team.

His third team was a constant problem for him. He tried switching them to different positions but problems always occurred. These horses would also create problems whenever they were placed in the other teams. It was difficult to understand why. They were all fit and healthy and of a similar ability, but they would constantly provoke one another. Raif had to separate them in the fields, as sometimes they would nip each other and cause mild skirmishes. He had to prevent this from happening, as injuries lowered performance even further. One of the horses was the worst offender, but she was a good lead horse as she had sound directional skills. Sometimes though, she would slacken off and needed to be reminded by the driver to keep up her speed. She would also bump the other lead horse to remind him that she was there. This would cause him to pull to one side, for which he was lashed by the driver. During their recreation it was payback time, as the other horses would find ways to push her out of the bran or nip her if they thought they could get away with it.

His fourth team was different again. This team had a wider range of abilities which Raif assumed must be the problem. The lead horses were enthusiastic and enjoyed responding to the driver. The rest of the team were left behind and struggled to keep up. The lead horses related well with those in the first and second teams but shied away from the third team. In the fields, the rest of the fourth team would run with third team and join in the nipping and nudging – something they never did when they were with their own team. This fourth team was quite successful and performed an above-average job. However, they could never really be a top team as some horses lacked commitment and would not pull their weight. They relied on the lead horses to do more than their fair share of work. The lead horses soon ignored the rest of the team and responded to the rewards given them by the drivers and passengers. This created resentment from the other team members. So out of harness, they sought the company of the third team horses.

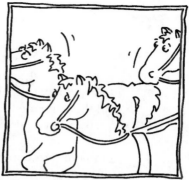

Team differences

An advertising company consisted of four main teams. The company was reasonably successful, but two of the teams were causing problems and this was impacting the organization.

The finance team was a small team which worked cooperatively in a quiet way. All had an eye for detail and the department ran smoothly. They had a focus on customer service and enjoyed the rewards of keeping the customers happy. They never interacted socially outside of work, but enjoyed each other's company during business hours. Their meetings were cordial and they shared the same vision and beliefs.

The sales team was motivated and successful. They understood and valued the different contributions that each person made to the team. They shared a high regard for one another and all celebrated their achievements. They would help each other with difficult prospects and when they achieved their 'stretch' targets they would gather for evening drinks to pat each other on the back. If there were any disagreements, they were soon resolved. They would meet regularly to discuss sales strategies and would share their contacts freely. They had learned that this openness led to outstanding results. All the team members had worked for the company for more than two years. Some had been there as long as five years, which was unusual for sales teams. They had found the recipe for success and their only problems arose in dealings with the production and marketing teams.

The production team was a bed of hot gossip and malcontent. Individually, each team member seemed well suited to the job and was reasonably efficient. The team leader tended to be autocratic in his dealings with the rest of the team and made it perfectly clear that he was boss. He had rigid ways of working and, as the longest-serving employee, thought that he knew best. His main assistant was a quiet, efficient young employee who worked in a neat and tidy way to complete the day's work. She had no ambition for promotion and was happy to do what the boss said. The other team members were slow workers and did the bare minimum to get by. They spent much of the day criticizing the leader and undermining his position. They loved creating rumours about the sales team as they were jealous of the high profile the team members received. There was no team spirit and all worked to meet their own needs, not the company's. When mistakes occurred, instead of learning from them and preventing their recurrence, they would be speedily rectified and hidden from management. Sometimes a customer might inform the general manager of a problem that had occurred, and this was an embarrassment to the team. Fortunately, though, most mistakes were able to be covered up.

The production team leader had been on several management and customer service courses. He usually returned brimming with ideas which never came to fruition, as it was too difficult to implement the change and easier to carry on as before. He tended to answer the telephone according to his mood, which varied throughout the day. Customer service started to decline and the level of complaints increased. Although the quality levels deteriorated, customers still liked the product and so sales were maintained and even increased. In meetings with the general manager, the production manager would take credit for the increased sales and never mention the quality and service problems that were occurring within his department. Instead, he would allude to problems in the other departments.

The marketing team was very enthusiastic and the team leaders were a mine of ideas and enthusiasm. They designed leaflets and

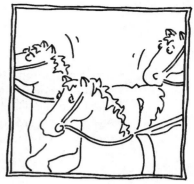

brochures to complement the products and their efforts brought in numerous leads for the sales team. They worked well with the finance and sales teams but had difficulties with the attitude in the production team, as it tended to be negative and defensive. The marketing team leaders were totally committed to the company and loved their work, but the rest of the team did not have the same motivation, as they were just there for the money. They indulged in a lot of gossip with the production team which didn't help the overall company morale. They complained about each other and never accepted responsibility for mistakes. It was always someone else's fault. The sales department would often complain about errors in the marketing leads, but the team leaders had difficulty in discovering the cause of the problem. The attitude of their team members discouraged them from probing any further. They preferred to rectify any problems themselves, rather than face the aggressive and defensive team members.

The general manager was most concerned about the variation in performance across his teams. It was time to take action and audit the problems before they affected the growth and profitability of the company.

Team management

The performance of teams varies greatly. Teams of some of the cleverest people can fail, whereas teams of below-average people can give above-average performance. What are the reasons for this?

Margerison and McCann (1995) have studied teams for over fifteen years and developed a model which helps explain why some management teams succeed and others fail. The answer lies in an understanding of individual work preferences and working patterns. As humans, we all have differing characteristics. If these characteristics are similar, individuals will often enjoy working together; if these characteristics are opposite, they may spend a lot of time in negative interactions. For example, outgoing people will often enjoy each another's company, chatting about all sorts of possibilities. However, an introverted person interacting with an extroverted person may describe him as 'loud-mouthed, waffling, and shallow', whereas the reverse criticism is often that the introvert is 'dull, boring and pedantic'. Given our human penchant for looking at others through negative 'glasses', it is not surprising that conflicts abound within teams.

The secret of high-performing teams is valuing the difference that individuals bring to a team and learning how to harness it positively.

Figure 3 The Margerison–McCann team management wheel ®

The Margerison–McCann team management wheel gives a model for understanding and working with differences. People can be classified as having work preferences in three or more parts of the wheel. These preferences then give an indication of the type of work they are likely to enjoy.

- **Reporter-advisers** enjoy gathering information and putting it together in a way that makes it easily understood. Usually they are patient people who prefer to have all the information before they take action.

- **Creator-innovators** enjoy thinking up new ideas and new ways of doing things. Usually they are very independent and will pursue their ideas regardless of existing systems and methods.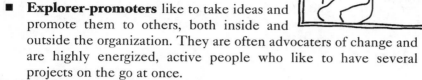
- **Explorer-promoters** like to take ideas and promote them to others, both inside and outside the organization. They are often advocaters of change and are highly energized, active people who like to have several projects on the go at once.
- **Assessor-developers** usually display a strong analytical approach and are at their best where several different possibilities need to be analysed and developed. They are often sociable, outgoing people who enjoy looking for new markets or opportunities.
- **Thruster-organizers** are people who enjoy making things happen. They are analytical decision makers, always doing what is best for the task, even if their actions sometimes upset others. Their great ability is to get things done, and for this reason they are often found working in project management positions.
- **Concluder-producers** are practical people who can be counted on to carry things through to the end. Their strength is in setting up plans and standard systems so that outputs can be achieved on a regular basis, in an orderly and controlled fashion.
- **Controller-inspectors** are quiet, reflective people who enjoy the detailed side of work, such as dealing with facts and figures. They are usually careful and meticulous and can spend long periods of time on a particular task, working quietly on their own.
- **Upholder-maintainers** are people with strong personal values and principles which are of prime importance in their decision making. Usually they have a high concern for people and will be strongly supportive of those who share the same ideals and values as they do.
- The **linker** role is a shared role that is held in conjunction with the other roles. It comprises eleven key skills focusing on the linking of people and the linking of tasks.

A successful team needs diversity and that is achieved by having a mixture of team role preferences. However, such a team will be in conflict unless everyone understands the different ways that individuals approach tasks. Making allowance for this and learning how to use different communication techniques with different people is the key to success.

In the book *How to Influence Others at Work* (McCann, 1993), guidelines for 'pacing' different parts of the team management wheel are given. These pacing techniques reduce conflict and contribute to cooperation and harmony. For example, when interacting with thruster-organizers some of the 'do's' and 'don'ts' are as follows:

Do's

- Be business-like and professional in interactions.
- Be factual.
- Focus on goals and outcomes.
- Be punctual.
- Summarize regularly (particularly the facts).

Don'ts

- Don't attack personally or be vague if you disagree with thruster-organizers. Point out in specific details how their course of action will cause negative results.
- Don't be ambiguous.
- Don't get off the subject.

Tips to improve teamwork

In the short term

- On a scale of 1 to 10, how would you rate your team?
- In terms of the team management wheel, what distributions of team roles do you have in your team? Are any roles missing? How might you plug the gaps?
- What level of conflict is there between team members? Opposites on the team management wheel have the most difficulty understanding each other because they see the world in different ways. Try explaining the concept of *pacing* to your team members.

In the longer term

- Consider introducing a programme of team development for your team. Developing a high-performing team is a process that takes considerable time. Start today by planning a year-long programme to get your team performance up to an optimal level.

Chapter Seventeen

Wolves

I N THE FROZEN NORTH of Canada, the snow was falling heavily as winter approached. The wolves knew that this could be their last chance to find food until spring, as already their prey were beginning to hibernate. Occasional tracks in the snow indicated that small mammals were scurrying about seeking their last meals. So at least there was still some food for the wolves to devour. The hibernating animals were lucky, as they could sleep through the winter, whereas the wolves had to continually hunt. The wolf pack would soon need to move south to follow the moose and deer.

The wolves were reluctant to leave their home. In the north were many caves where the pack could easily observe the surrounding countryside. Mating had occurred and cubs would arrive in the spring. They delayed their departure a little, as their caves here on the high ground were much more comfortable than those on the lower slopes. The birth of their young, the thaw and the return to their home was a strong incentive for survival through the winter. Their instinct for self-preservation made them even more aggressive as food was scarce this winter, after a poor summer.

Soon, regular fights broke out amongst the restless wolves. They hunted in small groups so that the prey could be surrounded. Slowly the wolves would move in, forcing the confused animal to bolt. One wolf was always close enough to lunge and capture the prey between his strong jaws. This strategy had worked well until this season, when all wolves were desperate for food. They would all make their move together, pushing one another out of the way. Many times the animal would escape and the wolves returned home cold and hungry.

The pack's move south was spoilt by this same aggressive behaviour. Continual fighting caused injuries and in their weak condition the wolves' wounds became easily infected. Many of them died during the long journey.

The leader of the pack became very worried and tried to discourage the in-fighting. He explained many times that unless the pack cooperated and shared the food, then they would all die. Still the fighting continued and every scrap of food was fought over.

The pack became very weak. Some of the females miscarried their young on route and a few even died from the stress. The leader spoke to each wolf individually, but still there was no change in behaviour.

Self-preservation prevailed. The leader made a decision to leave the pack with his two females to make a new life for themselves. At first some of the other wolves followed, but the leader fought them off and they backed away, not wanting to get lost in the snow. Tracks were difficult to follow and a lone wolf would surely perish.

Eventually the leader reached the lower plains where the moose and deer were grazing on the meagre grass and shrubs. Here the leader and his females settled down to survive the winter, ready to start a new pack in the spring. It would be a few years before they had the strength of numbers again, but the leader had learned from his experience and knew what was required to develop an effective pack. He would teach his offspring what he had learned and with his inherited characteristics, they would be well placed to eventually establish and lead their own pack. His blood line would be assured of survival.

Self-destruction

The brass foundry management team knew that to survive this take-over and keep their jobs, they would have to prove to their new owners they could run a brass company effectively. The purchasing company had no expertise in brass moulding, but had acquired the company as part of their vertical integration strategy. They were designers and wholesalers of home and garden products and many of their products were made of brass. This integration would fit well and hopefully provide some synergies in operation.

The new company was well known for its radical measures of staff performance and the consequences of not meeting those measures. Successful employees were rewarded handsomely; marginal employees were terminated. The pattern of previous take-overs was consistent. All jobs would be carefully reviewed and productivity gains implemented by staff reductions. As the managing director said, 'We are in business to make money, not hire losers.'

Rumours and gossip about redundancies were rife in the brass company. The general manager, Stanislav Taube had spoken to his team and assured them there was nothing to worry about, provided they concentrated on performance. He explained that the new company was interested in bottom-line outputs and paying attention to this was paramount to their survival.

The gossip and negativity continued unabated and, as a result, the outputs slowly decreased. Morale declined and no matter how often Stanislav explained that their jobs were safe, some members continued to undermine him and fuel the rumours. A few team members resigned and went to other jobs, rather than waiting to see what the new company would do. The ring leaders of the rumours were the least efficient in the team and had a reputation for 'fiddling the system' and spending longer than usual on meal breaks. Their current behaviour did nothing for their reputation or that of the company.

Stanislav felt that the team was tearing itself apart, for no apparent reason. It was almost as if certain members had a 'death wish' and he was worried that the team would become the victim of a self-fulfilling prophecy. Eventually Stanislav had no choice but to confront them and offer a redundancy package. It was the only way he could see to save his company.

This action gave the rebels a great deal of satisfaction and confirmed what they had been prophesying for months. Little did they realize that their behaviour had pre-determined the result. Had they worked together with the team towards the objective of improving bottom-line performance, their jobs would have been saved. Stanislav spent many sleepless nights over his decision, but he knew that he could work better with a few willing staff than with many disruptive ones.

The brass company take-over went ahead and Stanislav justified his action to the parent company in terms of efficiency gains. The reduced team lacked some expertise but between them they made up for shortfalls in their determination to succeed. Stanislav had built up the company from a shed in his garden and he didn't want to see his hard work die. His company name would be lost in the large conglomerate, but he could never lose his pride in a job well done.

Competition

A wolf pack is a very successful team when the wolves cooperate. They surround their prey so that there is no escape. The spoils are shared by all. Many teams in the business world today are similar 'hunting' teams. They are there to be competitive, to win. If they don't hunt down the prey, others will. In the cut and thrust of the corporate world, predators can easily become prey, unless they are consistently winning.

Successful sporting teams have that 'warrior' aspect as well. Witness the New Zealand All-Black rugby team, chanting its Maori war cry, prior to the match. Most international sporting teams have permanent sports psychologists employed to 'psyche up' the team for 'battle'. When they go out onto the field, they are there to hunt, to destroy the enemy.

As individuals, we all have a tremendous amount of psychic energy to expend. In a team this energy needs to be collectively channelled and focused on achieving pre-defined objectives. Once this energy is turned within, it will dissipate in useless 'in-fighting' or 'back-biting'.

Like the wolf pack, many team members turn on each other and tear themselves to pieces. The reasons are varied. Sometimes it is due to personality differences, sometimes to individual competition where several people are vying for the same few places at the top of the corporate pyramid.

We have all been a part of teams where there is petty conflict and a difference of opinion. In fact many of the high-performing teams we have worked with have this characteristic. When difficult decisions have to be made, it is important to present differing view points – what is technically called *multiple descriptions* of the same problem, solution

or opportunity. Multiple descriptions are more likely to occur in diverse teams where there is a mixture of different team role preferences. If every team member enjoys the same team role then a *single description* will occur, rather than multiple descriptions. For example, if all team members have a controller-inspector preference then it is more likely that the team will come up with a *controlling* solution to a problem. This can lead to what Irving Janis (1972) described many years ago as *group think*.

However, what makes high-performing teams different is their commitment to accept differing viewpoints and work them through by active listening, two-way communication and consultation. As soon as difference of opinion turns to negativity, energy is wasted on internal squabbling and that leaves less to focus on the 'prey'.

For a team to be successful there must be a high level of respect, understanding and trust. This is a very difficult aspect of teamwork to develop. Sometimes there is such a history of conflict and negativity, that no amount of intervention will fix things up. It is often best to apply radical surgery at an early stage, and like the wolf pack in our story re-form a new team and work hard there to establish a basis of TRUTH (trust, respect, understanding, teamwork, and honesty).

Tips to avoid team-destruction

In the short term

■ Consider to what extent your team engages in negative behaviour. If you consider it to be serious, then read the two stories in this chapter at your next team meeting. Ask the team to establish norms which might prevent this from happening.

In the longer term

■ Organize a team development programme for your team to discover the TRUTH. If improvements do not occur, then take the 'hard option' before it is too late. Wield your surgeon's knife!

Chapter Eighteen

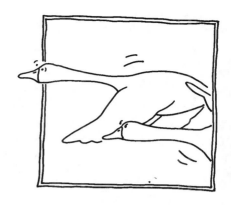

Geese

GEESE HAVE BEEN famous for their wonderful cooperation in flight, but not every gaggle of geese works well!

In the south of Norway, just outside the town of Bergen, lived an extended family of geese. They loved the clean, crisp mountain water and the abundant supply of food that each summer season brought. However, each goose had a different personality and far from cooperating with one another, there was a continual battle for supremacy.

They all wanted to be the leader and would constantly try to prove their superiority. They did not understand and value the different abilities that each goose brought to the colony. Each day they flew down to the lake and spent their time fossicking for food. Each evening they would return to the safety of the mountains. The battle for the lead began even before the flock was airborne, with a series of nips and digs to ensure that an advantage was gained in being the first to leave the ground. Whoever managed to take off first was leader for the journey. Despite almost fainting from exhaustion, the leader would never drop to the back to let another take over. This was a show of weakness and he would be jeered by the others if he relented.

Many of the older geese found this behaviour amusing. Why anyone would choose to take the lead all the time was a total mystery to them. It was the most strenuous position. 'Why do extra work if you don't need to?'

These battles raged for months. It wasn't until winter approached and the flock prepared for the journey south, that any change in behaviour occurred. When it was time for the migration, the flock gathered on the east bank of the lake and jostled for position. One of the quieter geese decided that it was time to show the strength he had been storing during the summer months. He flapped vigorously, thrusting his webbed feet across the surface of the lake. He was first into the air and gained the lead position.

The flight south was long and arduous. The warm breezes of summer were no longer there to give extra lift. The lead goose pushed forward strongly, creating a slip-stream behind him to suck the others forward. Pain flowed through his body but after trying all summer, he was now lead goose and wasn't giving that prize up easily. He persisted for as long as he could but fell away to the rear of the flock, eventually collapsing from exhaustion and plummetting into the sea. The other geese were momentarily distressed but another goose took over, anxious to prove what he could do. They lost their bearings for a while as the newcomer adapted to the leadership. Soon though, he fell back and also died from exhaustion.

Now it was time for one of the older, wiser geese to take over. He moved to the front position and stayed there for only an hour or so, before he dropped to the rear and asked one of his friends to take over. This rotation set the example and the younger geese began to experience the benefits of teamwork. The flight was so much easier when the load was shared. The stubbornness of the first two geese had led to their death, but they were merely adhering to the culture that had become an unwritten law in this gaggle of geese. It was a hard lesson to learn, when they could so easily have developed an efficient, cooperative group culture during those summer months in Bergen. Life is hard enough without struggling to make it more difficult!

Jostling for position

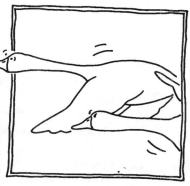

Although the managing director was often in the office, the senior managers of the stockbroking company, Morgan Associates, made all the decisions without consultation. It was the way the MD liked it, as she was more interested in her board duties in Morgans and for the other companies in which she was a director. Marie Le Feuvre was pleased with her senior management team as the figures always looked good. She rarely spoke to them, apart from the quarterly meetings where just one senior manager would address the board. It was a different member each time and this pleased Marie as it showed that the self-directed team which she had encouraged, was working.

However, behind the scenes, the quarterly meetings were a source of competition. Each of the managers desperately wanted to be the one to present the results to the Board and to represent the team. This caused tension and fighting amongst the managers as they jostled for position, almost as soon as the last board meeting was finished. They had discussed a rotation scheme, but had rejected it because each manager thought that he or she was the best equipped to represent the team. So the arguments raged every three months as each person put forward their case to be chosen for the next meeting.

The team had a shared goal of maximizing profits, but competition rather than cooperation prevailed. They had all been used to managing subordinate staff in previous positions and these ingrained patterns constantly showed up in the way each one pushed to 'score points' over the others.

Any mistakes that occurred were used as weapons to blame others and reduce their influence in the group. Behaviour of this sort would change the pecking order in the team, affecting the chances of being selected to present at the next board meeting. Everyone wanted to maximize their chance of being selected as the next MD, and the best way of doing this was to present to the board. Therefore any opportunity to sabotage one another's projects was taken and Marie was always told of any failures. Usually the only opportunity to do this was in the preliminary discussions she held with the quarterly presenter prior to the board meeting. Marie was so busy that it was difficult to see her at others times and she rarely read, in depth, any of the written correspondence.

The senior management team all had very different personalities. Some were very action oriented and quick to make decisions, whereas others spent time sifting through information and delayed decisions. This was a source of irritation and when their weekly meetings came around, conflict usually occurred. Time was spent in arguing and decisions were made in haste due to lack of time for sensible discussion.

The strain became too much for the research manager and he suffered a heart attack which put him in hospital and off work for three months. His deputy replaced him and was amazed at the conflict within the group. It was only when the finance manager was admitted to hospital with a ruptured stomach ulcer, that the team decided to look at itself. The two deputies helped a great deal in this as they could see the problems from a different perspective. Their meetings became less aggressive and eventually they all settled down to work together, instead of destroying one another's health in a fruitless, competitive battle.

Self-directed teams

Being a leader is not about demonstrating 'position' power, although many managers still act like the gaggle of geese! While it is important for a leader to set an example, it is not necessary for a leader to always 'be in charge'. Work is so complex these days that it is impossible for one person to always know what is right. That is why teams exist. By working together, a team has the capability of regularly making the right decision, but only if the leader understands his or her limitations. Assigning tasks according to an individual's capabilities and preferences and then empowering them to take decisions and implement results is one of the characteristics of a high-performing team.

Self-directed teams are increasingly being formed in many organizations. These have no clearly-defined leader and the teams work cooperatively to achieve goals which are set for them. By flying in a 'V' formation a flock of geese creates an uplift which adds 70 per cent to its flying range. Similarly a self-directed team shares a common direction and a sense of belonging and is carried along by the synergy of the individual efforts.

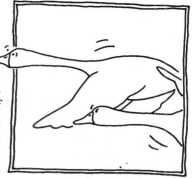

Whenever a goose falls out of formation, it will experience the extra drag of flying alone. This is enough to encourage it to become part of the group again. So if we have our own personal goals it may sometimes be wiser to team up with others who are headed where we want to go.

When a goose feels ill or is wounded, two geese will drop out of formation and follow the sick goose downwards, providing protection where necessary until the goose recovers or dies. Likewise team members in an ideal self-directed team will stand by one another when adverse circumstances occur.

Self-directed teams are popular in many business process reengineering (BPR) interventions. Here 'process' teams are formed to focus on customers. Customers want instant service and the teams to service them consist of a cross-functional mixture of, for example, sales people, accountants, technical experts, and so on. Any problem a customer has can be solved using the resources available within the team. In conventional organizational structures, delays and mistakes often occur when several departmental boundaries have to be crossed in servicing a customer. These cross-functional teams also have a high level of empowerment to avoid delays when decisions are passed to supervisors for approval. So with BPR goes the process of 'flatter structures' where layers of management are removed and team members are empowered to make their own decisions.

For self-directed teams to work well, there must be a substantial investment in training and development. Problems have occurred in many organizations where the 'empowerment light switch' is used ...'click', now you are empowered! Self-directed teams require a high level of self understanding and need to quickly establish group norms so that procedures are available when problems and difficulties arise.

In a self-directed team the concept of 'linking' is important (Margerison and McCann, 1995). Linking is a process of integrating both people and tasks and is a skill that all team members should implement. Skills which contribute to the linking of people are active listening, communication, problem solving and counselling, team relationships, interface management and participative decision making. Skills which contribute to the linking of tasks are: work allocation, team development, delegation, objective setting and quality standards.

A self-directed team must also be a learning team. A certain level of humility helps, where team members realize their current limitations but are committed to life-long learning. Many members of highly successful self-directed teams continually update their skills by regularly attending development workshops or by distance learning. A programme of individual learning will flow over into a culture of group learning.

Learning from mistakes is one of the most important group learning processes. When people make mistakes they need to know they will not be punished, provided they are open about the error and are prepared to freely discuss how it occurred. Discussion should then centre around what procedures might be established to prevent this mistake from occurring again.

Tips for self-directed teams

In the short term

■ As a leader, consider how you can help your team to become more self-directed. Like the flock of geese, work out ways to develop interdependency in your team. Tasks should be shared and leadership rotated according to the situation.

■ Review how well your team is 'linked'. Do team members respect, understand and trust one another? How well are individual tasks and objectives linked with the team objectives. Are there common goals amongst team members?

■ Consider what procedures you have in place to facilitate learning from mistakes.

In the longer term

Examine the potential for self-directed teams in your organization. Gather as much information as you can by reading and talking with others. How might you reengineer your organization for improved results? With self-directed teams there could be a potential for improved productivity.

Finale

We would like to finish the book with two stories which have become personal favourites. Our communication workshops are usually concluded with both of these stories. The first one is another story from *The Forest People* (Turnbull, 1961) and often strikes a chord with participants, particularly those caught up in the 'corporate' world. It describes Kenge dancing:

> One night in particular will always live for me, because that night I think I learned just how far we civilized human beings have drifted from reality. The moon was full, so the dancing had gone on for longer than usual. Just before going to sleep I was standing outside my hut when I heard a curious noise from the nearby children's bopi. This surprised me, because at night-time the Pygmies generally never set foot outside the main camp. I wandered over to see what it was.
>
> There, in the tiny clearing, splashed with silver, was the sophisticated Kenge, clad in bark cloth, adorned with leaves, with a flower stuck in his hair. He was all alone, dancing around and singing softly to himself as he gazed up at the treetops.

Now Kenge was the biggest flirt for miles, so, after watching a while, I came into the clearing and asked, jokingly, why he was dancing alone. He stopped, turned slowly around and looked at me as though I was the biggest fool he had ever seen; and he was plainly surprised by my stupidity.

'But I am *not* dancing alone,' he said. 'I am dancing with the forest, dancing with the moon.' Then, with the utmost unconcern, he ignored me and continued his dance of love.

The second story is self-explanatory. It highlights many of the problems we face in both our work and private lives. It is an extract from the book *The Heart is the Hunter*, by Laurens Van der Post (1961).

This man of the early race dearly loved his black and white cattle. He always took them out into the veldt himself, chose the best possible grazing for them, and watched over them like a mother over her children, seeing that no wild animals came near to hurt or disturb them. In the evening he would bring them back to his kraal, seal the entrance carefully with branches of the toughest thorn, and watching them contentedly chewing the cud, think, 'In the morning I shall have a wonderful lot of milk to draw from them.' One morning, however, when he went into his kraal expecting to find the udders of the cows full and sleek with milk, he was amazed to see they were slack, wrinkled and empty. He thought, with immediate self-reproach, he had chosen their grazing badly, and took them to better grass. He brought them home in the evening and again thought, 'Tomorrow for a certainty I shall get more milk than ever before.' But again in the morning the udders were slack and dry. For the second time he changed their grazing, and yet again the cows had no milk. Disturbed and suspicious, he decided to keep a watch on the cattle throughout the dark.

In the middle of the night he was astonished to see a cord of finely-woven fibre descending from the stars; and down this cord, hand over hand, one after another, came some young women of the people of the sky. He saw them, beautiful and gay, whispering and laughing softly among themselves, steal into the kraal and milk his cattle dry with calabashes. Indignant, he jumped out to catch them but they scattered cleverly so that he did not know which way to run. In the end he did manage to catch one; but while he was chasing her the rest, calabashes and all, fled up the sky, withdrawing

Aesop's Management Fables

the cord after the last of them so that he could not follow. However, he was content because the young woman he had caught was the loveliest of them all. He made her his wife and from that moment he had no more trouble from the women of the people of the sky.

His new wife now went daily to work in the field for him while he tended his cattle. They were happy and they prospered. There was only one thing that worried him. When he caught his wife she had a basket with her. It was skilfully woven, so tight that he could not see through it, and was always closed firmly on top with a lid that fitted exactly into the opening. Before she would marry him, his wife had made him promise that he would never lift the lid of the basket and look inside until she gave him permission to do so. If he did a great disaster might overtake them both. But as the months went by, the man began to forget his promise. He became steadily more curious, seeing the basket so near day after day, with the lid always firmly shut. One day when he was alone, he went into his wife's hut, saw the basket standing there in the shadows, and could bear it no longer. Snatching off the lid, he looked inside. For a moment he stood there unbelieving, then burst out laughing.

When his wife came back in the evening, she knew at once what had happened. She put her hand to her heart, and looking at him with tears in her eyes, she said, 'You've looked in the basket.'

He admitted it with a laugh, saying, 'You silly woman. You silly, silly creature. Why have you made such a fuss about this basket? There's nothing in it at all.'

'Nothing?' she said, hardly finding the strength to speak.

'Yes, nothing,' he answered emphatically.

At that she turned her back on him, walked away straight into the sunset and vanished. She was never seen on earth again.

A thought for everyone

Stories are written for education and pleasure;
Read and learn for business as well as for leisure.

References

Bettelheim, B. (1976) *The Uses of Enchantment: the meaning and importance of fairy tales*. Thames and Hudson, London.

Blyton, E. (1984; originally published in 1939) *The Enchanted Wood*. Budget Books, Melbourne.

Churchill, Winston, (1968) *The Wartime Speeches of Winston Churchill 1939–1945*. The Decca Recording Company, London.

Hirose, N. (1992) *Immovable Wisdom – The Art of Zen Strategy*. Element Books, Shaftesbury.

Honey, P. and Mumford, A. (1982) *The Manual of Learning Styles*. Peter Honey, Ardingly House, 10 Linden Avenue, Maidenhead.

Janis, I. (1972) *Victims of Group Think*. Houghton Mifflin, New York.

Mandela, N. (1994) *Long Walk to Freedom*. Abacus, Little Brown & Co, London.

Mathews, J. (1994) *The Opal that Turned into Fire*. Magabala Books Aboriginal Corporation, Broome, Western Australia.

McCann, D. (1993) *How to Influence Others at Work*. 2nd edition, Butterworth-Heinemann, Oxford.

Margerison, C. and McCann, D. (1995a) *Team Management – Practical New Approaches*. Management Books 2000, Didcot, UK.

Margerison, C. and McCann, D. (1995b) *Team Reengineering – Using the Language of Teamwork*. Team Management Systems, York and Brisbane.

Phillips, B. (1996) Future mapping: a practical way to map out the future and achieve what you want. *Career Development International*, Vol. 1, No. 8, MCB University Press, Bradford.

Senge, P., Roberts, C., Ross, R., Smith, B. and Kleiner, A. (1994) *The Fifth Discipline Fieldbook*, Nicholas Brealey, London.

Shah, I. (1990) *The Way of the Sufi*. Arkana Books, London.

Turnbull, C. (1961) *The Forest People*. Johnathan Cape, London.

Van der Post, L. (1961) *The Heart is the Hunter*. Hogarth Press, London.

Stories for learning

If you would like to attend a workshop to develop your skills in creating stories for learning, please contact Jan Stewart at the following numbers:

UK workshops: Telephone and fax: 01904 701023
Australian workshops: Telephone: 0412 234412 Fax: 07 3368 2311

Workshops are held throughout the year for trainers and teachers who want to create learning stories to use with their students. Workshops are also held for people interested in creating stories for use in educating family members, especially children.